Ordinary Oneness

The Simplicity of Everyday Love, Grace and Hope

Compiled by Kyra Schaefer

Ordinary Oneness: The Simplicity of Everyday Love, Grace and Hope

As You Wish Publishing, LLC
Connect@asyouwishpublishing.com
www.asyouwishpublishing.com

ISBN-13: 978-1-951131-17-3

Library of Congress Control Number: 2021905742

Printed in the United States of America.

Nothing in this book or any affiliations with this book is a substitute for medical or psychological help. If you are needing help please seek it.

Dedication

To those of you dearest ones who lost so much in this life to find that your grace wasn't in the having, but in the losing. You recognize a simple beauty all around you. You have, as Osho says, fallen together. It is the soft delicate snowflakes, the gentle movement of trees in the wind; it's the daily chores done consciously and peacefully which make up the entirety of our lives. These are the moments that help us know ourselves and the world better.

Peace rests gently in the ordinary.

Table of Contents

Listen, See, Know and Be
By Anne Foster Angelou

First of all, there is nothing ordinary about oneness. In fact, it's extraordinary in every way. When you think, as I do, about oneness, including every living being—human or animal—and our precious Mother Earth, it's quite amazing.

When we humans are functioning from the heart center, we love and forgive. We share, care and feel deeply about each other. Intellectual and creative abilities aside, we feel joy or sadness with a wide range of intensity for both. The emotions of fear, anger, guilt and shame happen to all of us. Some of us are avoiders, and others are "head-on" copers. Bring it on! Let's get this solved so everyone's needs are met. It's a fine aspiration, but as life goes, it doesn't always happen that way.

As a child, I remember being shy and often fearful, but it was commensurate with what was happening around me. I still laughed, played, enjoyed dolls, toys and board games, and had an active fantasy life about being an exotic belly dancer and Tarzan's Jane. I leaped out of trees with an imaginary dagger in my hand, defending some equally imaginary cause or immediate peril. I prayed and attended Catholic Mass, where I sang Gregorian chant and other liturgical music. I remember feeling so angelic with my hands clasped and eyes closed, trying my little girl's best to reach the Divine. We were more reverent in those days when only whispers were allowed, and the quiet, solemnity and ritual were a comforting promise of better days to come with relief from drama, immediacy, emergency and even hunger.

Oneness? Circumstances did change for the better. Someone came, and something happened for blessed relief. Humans can be so kind and beautifully helpful. They are ready to share tears and laughter, to hug and comfort. Thank God!

I learned by example from a very poor, melancholy but zany and spontaneous grandmother how to love, forgive, persevere, hope, be courageous and make a difference in my life and the lives of others. I don't remember when I thought of only myself, especially in my early life. I had some "Mount Vesuvius" type meltdowns during meno-pause, but I don't wish to use hormones as an excuse. Remember the 10-second rule.

It is oneness when you see someone crying, and you feel it deeply in your heart when you go to them immediately to hug or say, "It's going to be okay." It's oneness when you don't want another person to hurt or be deprived of the basics to survive or thrive. It's oneness when humans rush to the scene of a natural disaster, risking their lives to save others and restore their homes. It's oneness when you donate for feeding and housing the poor, for social justice issues or for animal rescue and sanctuary because you feel a financial contribution is the least you can offer. It is oneness when you do not harm the Earth. A poisoned, dying Earth cannot support human life. Oneness is knowing, caring and doing something about it.

Ordinary Oneness

I attended a 10-week class at The Center for Spiritual Living called "Beyond Limits." In the last class, we were instructed to divide into two; half of us in the center and the rest of us outside waiting to enter. "Do not speak or touch. Look into each one's eyes and realize you are looking upon the face of God." Oneness is why we sobbed, looking at each other. Gazing steadily with vulnerability will quickly synchronize your hearts and souls. It was powerful. We must remember our oneness as we encounter each person whose struggles we cannot know.

A sense of oneness can help prevent an emotional meltdown, hysteria, and very bad choices that will surely harm and sadden someone unnecessarily. I heard, "God's job would be so much easier if we all knew each other's thoughts." Love and forgiveness are always the best choices. As much as I know myself as a compassionate and generous person, my lifetime mistakes are many and regrettable. Still, we cannot torture ourselves needlessly with guilt. Maya Angelou said, "When we know better, we do better." I am grateful to have been given more chances to make different choices. Coming from a place of love feels so much better.

Oneness is much more challenging when violence and danger are involved. We must realize that many humans are mentally ill, poorly nurtured and deprived of basic needs, or steeped in a life of crime. I don't like the saying, "There, but for the grace of God, go I," because it sounds like God is pulling strings and deliberately allowing harm for some and not for others. I don't believe God, or the Divine/ Source takes sides. We have that wonderful gift called "free will." We can be the change we wish to see in the world, as Gandhi said.

Dare I say it is oneness when we gather publicly and peacefully to protest injustice and insist on change. It is our oneness that will not allow racism, misogyny, cruelty, genocide, domestic or sexual violence, homophobia or discrimination of any kind to prevail. United we stand, divided we fall. I celebrate all races, faiths, cultures, countries, and languages that are part of this beautiful world. By a circumstance of birth, I was born into an American Christian/Catholic family. There are many paths to the same end. I say truth depends on what you were taught and the choices you make. For our physical bodies, it is said that we are made of "the stuff of stars," and I believe it. True or not, I also heard that the chemical composition of our bodies is the same as soil or the Earth. "Remember man that thou art dust and to dust thou shalt return." Every morning I wake up is a blessing and another chance to make a difference. Sometimes I'll get it right, and other times, I won't. A wise teacher said, "There is very little difference between the Saint and the Sinner."

"Happiness is giving up the need to: (1) control others, (2) judge others, and (3) to be right." I don't know the author, but I'm putting it in quotation marks because they are not my ideas even though I like them and try to live by them.

Without heart-pounding details, a significant trauma occurred when my age 19, seven months pregnant Aunt "J" came to live with us when I was eight. She suffered extreme spousal abuse—physical, mental and sexual—until she "snapped" (psychotic depression). Thankfully, out of the oneness, she received medical care, divorced, and slowly recovered over several years to live a long life. The witnessing has been etched in my memory. My grandmother took care of my aunt and cousin until Little "J" was four. She raised me to age 19.

In those days, kind and generous strangers brought us food in response to a plea posted on a public bulletin board. The bus driver let us ride for free if we boarded at the end of the line because he knew we were poor and on our way to church, many miles away.

Months after Aunt "J" came to live with us, my grand-mother, Little "J" and I went to visit my mother and her third husband, John, in New York City and witnessed a violent, drunken brawl in the apartment. The police came and tended to me, the baby and my grandmother after the arrests. My youngest Aunt "H," 17 years old and a visiting dancer on tour, went to the ER and survived the beating. I spent the night being rocked in my grandmother's arms, trying not to see the huge blood spatters on the walls. She had taught me to sing, so she urged me to sing one of her favorite songs to distract me, "Alice Blue Gown." The last note was high and always challenging. She encouraged me to try, so I sang it. The incident was days before my 9th birthday.

Where was the oneness here? It was the police, medical staff, and apartment neighbors we didn't know but who came and cared. Weeks before the brawl, John told us to leave, and we had no lodging, so we visited the Museum of Natural History during the day and slept at the Greyhound Station at night—my grandmother, the baby and me. He put most of our belongings on the front step just as the garbage was being collected. We watched them being chewed up by the compactor. I'm sure the staff in both places did not know we were temporarily homeless. They were part of the oneness, greeting us each day and tending to our visitors' needs. Fortunately, the judge, challenging my grandmother's guardianship and my being exposed to violence, allowed her to keep me and return home to Tampa, Florida when he was assured we would not remain in that environment.

For the rest of my life from age 19, when I left home in 1963 and crossed the country alone, kind souls came from the oneness to let me know they were there for me or a beloved. My life was prolonged in 2013 by medical staff and surgery that treated hypertrophic cardiomyopathy undiagnosed for 15 years. God bless the Mayo Clinic, Rochester, MN.

I have found oneness in the performing arts among beloved singer and musician colleagues, an expression of my heart and soul. "I get by with a little help from my friends." They were there for my separation, divorce and depression in my 20s. I have also returned the love for friends who suffered depression and survived not wanting to live anymore. Thank God for the oneness, the knowing, the shared compassion, and being there.

We are all on a similar path, and the journey's end will be alone. I am grateful we have helping hands and hearts along the way to bear our struggles more easily, to live with courage and hope, realizing we are all one and that love and forgiveness are the only choices. Those who make harmful choices for themselves and others need even more love and prayers. Express them freely. Open your hearts and pray for everyone, even if you must keep a safe distance. There is no special training for prayer. Just close your eyes, focus on your heart center, and include all life in your healing and happy intentions. You don't have to be in a house of worship. Wherever you are is perfect. It's up to us as individuals, and together we can do this. Separation, the opposite of oneness, is what causes our pain. Reach out your hand, smile with love, and remember the oneness. We are not what or whom we know, have or experience. We are not our credentials or resumé. We are the love we give. "It is in giving that we receive...." Let's live this wonderful life in harmony, finding joy in others. Let us laugh, play, dance and sing along with all the serious and responsible things we must do. Thank you for being in my world. We are all imperfect, and that's okay. Do your best and know that, in difficulty, "this too shall pass." Invite blessings on your body's cells with golden light and healing. Take care of your temple. Forgive someone and heal both of you. I have been blessed to share my life for the last 48 years with a loving and wonderful partner. In our respective personal experiences, we have known the life-saving oneness. See the Divine in all beings, and don't forget to love.

Bio

Anne lives in Seattle, WA, with her native-born Greek husband of 48 years, and has lived a long, interesting life full of joy and many challenges. She was blessed with experience in the performing arts from childhood and has yearned to write her "stories" since the age of 30. She enjoys humor, laughter and meeting other people whose stories further enhance her knowledge of what life is all about. Anne enjoys writing, other people's talent and accomplishments, cats, and learning something new each day. Seeing other people happy is a great joy. Email: fosterangelou@comcast.net.

Enough is a Feast
By Megan Arthurs

We live in a world where we constantly seek more. More money, more likes, more food, more love, more praise, more materialism. But how do we know when enough is enough? How do we know when enough has become too much? In the search for everyday love, grace, and hope, we need to stop searching. What we are seeking is right in front of us; we are merely missing one integral component to show us that what we have is enough: gratitude.

The term gratitude has become increasingly popular in the 21st century. However, the practice behind the term often gets lost. Holidays, gift-receiving, and gratitude journals are reminders that there is a reason to be thankful and show appreciation for what we have. However, when we only show thanks during a few holidays a year, what we have will never be enough. The ratio of mundane days to holidays does not equate to a year full of gratitude, but rather a few fleeting moments. This is why gratitude needs to be something expressed daily. It needs to be part of our lifestyle, it needs to become more than a 30-page journal, it needs to seep into our very being at the soul level.

When we choose to stand in a place of gratitude, we can turn a meal into a feast. A stare into a smile. A house into a home. A ripple into a wave. When we practice gratitude and live in gratitude, we will constantly be surrounded by everyday love, grace, and hope. We will not have to chase after it—it will find us, it will be who we are as people, a collective society filled with gratitude.

Gratitude is not exclusively a list of things to be thankful for; it is a muscle we need to awaken and learn how to activate so we can truly embody and acknowledge what it means to be grateful from the moment we rise to the time we rest. Grateful for what we have, grateful for one another, and grateful for our journey in an increasingly noisy world.

Gratitude is an energetic shift in how we behave in the world. It turns what we have into enough. It forces us to become incredibly present, to live in the moment and let go of all troubles past and all troubles yet to come. In this state, we can notice the little things and constantly look for the good, even in unpleasant situations. When we learn to rejoice in the small and ordinary, we surrender to our complaints and create space for everyday good fortune.

What do we gain from a feast anyway? Is it reassurance that we will be full? Does it make us happier, healthier, kinder, or more loving? Our source of joy does not come from an amount of something that is more than necessary, but rather from the small and ordinary. Knowing that there is no value in excess and no voids to fill, we will naturally feel enough, feel we have enough, and feel worthy of everything we desire.

Integrating a life full of gratitude means we must start each day with a grateful heart and positive thoughts. Acknowledging that every morning when our feet hit the ground, we are given a gift, another day. The thoughts we feed ourselves throughout the day become our reality. If we want a hopeful future, we must speak to ourselves with optimism, love, and compassion. Our mindsets are central to our health and behavior, as our thoughts help manifest our future desires. If we constantly think negatively, we will continually see negative things, be surrounded by negative people, and endure negative experiences. When we let go of what is seemingly negative to us (big or small), what we are left with is space to focus on truth, beauty, and goodness. This will anchor us in gratitude.

We surround ourselves with positive people and environments. If you hang around five confident people, you will be the sixth. If you hang around five millionaires, you will be the sixth. If you hang around five ungrateful people, you will be the sixth. With whom and where we choose to spend our time has a direct influence on who we are becoming. Every day we have the choice to become someone better than we were yesterday. We get to choose who we allow into our lives and what roads we take our-selves on. The environment in which we immerse ourselves reflects our inner spiritual space. It can influence our thoughts and actions. When we leave certain people or places and feel a low vibration, there is something that needs to shift. This type of relationship or environment is toxic to our well-being and will drown the idea of gratitude. We must choose our surroundings and tribe wisely.

We bring gratitude to our experiences instead of waiting for a positive experience to feel grateful. If we are always waiting for the wins in life to spark joy within us, we will miss the small, tender times that are more meaningful. All we have to do is play the game; winning is not essential for growth and happiness. Finding little joys in the expected will bring more bliss to us than that car, raises, a new handbag. Bringing gratitude with you into your routine means appreciating the rain as much as the sun. Finding light in little setbacks, understanding that frustration is a way for you to slow down and learn a lesson. It's common to react negatively and become emotional when life throws us roadblocks and detours. We become quick-tempered, frustrated, angry, and annoyed. Why? It's truthfully much less painful and exhausting if we find gratitude even in our darkest moments. In every situation, if you pause and look for the light—you'll find it. It will be shining down on you. Let it shine all the time, let it shine!

We bring more compassion, love, and empathy to the world through our engagement and action in the work we do and how we carry ourselves throughout the day. Our contribution exists through our hobbies and career, which attaches to a lineage that pays homage to our past and influences our future. We should always participate with warm-heartedness, understanding, and care. When you lead with love and kindness, you will always leave people better than you found them. We must put love and compassion forward in our careers, our peers, our family, and most importantly, to those with whom we are unacquainted with. When you dance your way through life with a full and helping heart, you will soon realize that universal love will come straight back to you.

We do what's right when no one is looking. Acting like a good citizen on occasion versus being a good citizen are two contrasting ideas. If every person did a little better when no one was looking, think about how the world would change. This includes how we treat one another, how we care for the environment, our thoughts, behaviors, and self-compassion.

We get involved. Getting involved allows us to discover our interests. We develop more skill and confidence, we help others, we learn, we grow, we become part of a community greater than the one we came from. There is no finer gift than being part of a community, and this is why we feel so vibrant when we go to a concert, church, a yoga class, or volunteer. When we immerse ourselves in a group of people that share common attitudes, interests, and goals, we come back to ourselves. From this place, we are better able to cultivate gratitude.

We educate ourselves on people and places in the world that are dissimilar to us. The more we understand others' situations, the more compassionate we become. In times of struggle, it is important to remind ourselves that someone may be experiencing challenging hardships similar or more painful to ours. We need this reminder to humble ourselves, to ground ourselves, and realize that we are never given something in life that we cannot handle, and we are certainly not alone. There are many common bonds we share with those close to us and those we will never get the pleasure to meet.

We live an authentic life with integrity that aligns with our highest principles. Living authentically means always living up to our values and morals and not someone else's. We lead with honesty, fairness, transparency, and good virtue. Living authentically means trusting our intuition, that little voice inside nudging us in various directions. That is our guiding compass, an all-knowing conductor leading us to the best destination we have yet to see. We must listen and connect to this voice as it will help us live a life full of sincerity.

Through these practices, we can mine our gratitude pursuit, which brings us closer to our desires. These actions will organically steer us to a daily reflection: what can I appreciate today that I normally overlook? What will your gratitude practice look like? Will you slow down, pause, and take in life's small glimpses of beauty? Will you volunteer? Will you bring more compassion into your professional life? Will you begin surrounding yourself with people that share similar values and morals to yours? Whatever you do, do it with love. Do it because you are stepping into gratitude, you are becoming grateful, you are embodying gratefulness.

2020 has been a challenging year for everyone, however, it has been a year of learning, growing, gratitude, and perspective. Without a strong sense of gratitude, it may have been more challenging for some. This was not the year to get everything we wanted and for all to go as planned, but it truly was the year to appreciate everything we have.

Perspective is everything. Have you ever heard of the saying, 'one man's trash is another man's treasure'? The differentiation between trash versus treasure is perspective. How we choose to view life is up to our free will. We get to decide how to show up, how to react, and how to behave. It is our frame of mind to declare what is trash and what is treasure. When we broaden our scope and view situations that come into our lives less personal, we can shift our perspective. This means we can judge less and love more.

This means we understand where other people are coming from because we can reflect on situations with multiple points of view. This means we forgive. This means we are grateful for the lesson and experience. This means we know better so we can do better next time. This is pure human growth. This is what it means to give thanks, without the pumpkin pie.

Gratitude makes sense of our past, brings peace for today, and creates a vision for tomorrow. It unlocks a door to the fullness of life. It surrounds us with everyday love, grace, and hope. It brings the fruits of life to us. It turns judgment into love, unkindness into grace, and despair into hope. When we are genuinely grateful, we experience happiness, joy, and pleasure at a deep soul level. We stop seeking far beyond a four-letter word because what we need is not more.

What we have is enough.

No need for seconds.

Bio

Megan Arthurs is a Professional Home Organizer and is the founder and owner of H:OM ORGANIZING. Megan believes organizing is a pillar to your optimal health and well-being, as the art of organization provides relief from mentally managing too many responsibilities. She is passionate about helping people transform and declutter their homes, which inevitably elevates and renews their life. Megan understands that you are fed by your environment—you can either be filled with joy, energy, peace, and inspiration or drained from it. She encourages her clients to find the OM in their home and life! Megan is a former dance teacher with a Master of Arts Degree in Dance. She is also a Certified Wedding Planner with a WPICC certificate. In her personal time, Megan is devoted to fitness, fresh air, fashion, spiritual growth, love, and kindness. You can reach Megan at info@homorganizing.ca / www.homorganizing.ca.

Healing in Ordinary Ways Through an Extraordinary Time
By Aileen Balizado, MA

"Joy is not a constant. It comes to us in moments—often ordinary moments. Sometimes we miss out on the bursts of joy because we are too busy chasing down extraordinary moments. Other times we are so afraid of the dark that we don't dare to let ourselves enjoy the light." —Dr. Brené Brown, *The Gifts of Imperfection.*

What a journey this has been during this unprecedented time in our history: a global pandemic, a change of political leadership, continuing civil unrest, racial division, protests—and we are all still in the journey from different vessels, in the same world. All over our planet, every human life was altered from newborn to elderly. This year of 2020, I find myself in the middle of life's journey.

This is my chapter to share how healing occurred for me in ordinary ways during this extraordinary time. When my office was closed due to Covid-19, my work from home life began. I have the blessing and challenge to live with my elderly parent and adult brother, sharing caregiving responsibilities and living a life I never would have imagined for myself. Previously, I had lost my place of employment in Los Angeles, where I lived independently for more than 25 years. When that division closed, however, I was fortunate to be able to move back to my hometown of Tempe, Arizona and transfer my position within my same company. This allowed me to keep my tenure and benefits and remain gainfully employed but now relocated to my previous hometown. It was a call to start over again, and I resisted.

How do I find a community to relate to? So many things came at me. My body was such a mess with incredible residual lower back pain from a previous L5-S1 discectomy requiring physical therapy. I joined a support group of injured patients working with an incredible group of personal trainers who gave us their time and energy freely, dedicated to providing group meetings and healing and wellness free of charge. It was a non-profit which no longer exists but was a basis of connecting me to other healers, of which I would later affectionately refer to as lightworkers—those who bring healing light in this world.

Now I know there are many more healers and lightworkers all around me. I am a devoted self-described self-care nerd. I have taken courses and webinars in Mindfulness-Based Stress Reduction, Yoga, Pilates, Dance, Warrior Sword Wielding, Drum Circles, Meditation Sound Baths, Cutting Cords, Space Clearing and Aroma Therapy. Sign me up! I needed respite and relief from working full time professionally and at-home caregiving.

During one of the sessions a guest speaker, Maya Nahra, Registered Dietician, DAIS, spoke to us about her self-discovery of how habits and behavior changes got her back to her health. It was like she was speaking to my heart and soul about her journey with food. It was beyond emotional eating, thinking, feeling and hearing about how my back pain was inflamed due to being incredibly overweight. I have since been committed to learning the teachings of Nuuaria Wellness (www.nuuaria.com) since 2017, so honored to be considered as a founding member in Heart Training. The tipping point for me was when I attended a retreat in Cave Creek and met my mentor and coach, Lori Monty, Mentor and Certified Nuuaria Method Trainer, founder of the Nuuaria Freedom program. This started a nine-month journey of curriculum and coaching calls from March 2020 until December 2020, focusing on experiences of emotional eating. This work has helped me connect to my higher self with awareness and loving support. I have released 25 lbs.

I have always been an avid student of life. I love to learn and have completed a Master's Degree in Clinical Psychology with a concentration in Organizational Development. I have also completed courses in transformational learning with Landmark Education and just completed the Curriculum for Living.

When the world was shutting down in Spring 2020, and I was practicing social distancing, my body began breaking down as well. This time it was not my back but instead my reproductive organs. My condition, adenomyosis, left me in so much pain, and I elected surgical removal—a hysterectomy. I was headed for the second surgery of my life and fortunately had the best team at Mayo Clinic to perform the surgery and care.

In August of 2020, I began a seminar with Landmark Education (www.landmarkworldwide.com) called Self Expression and Leadership. Over 40 participants, including myself, created our own community projects where over 9,000 people in the US and internationally could benefit from what we created.

In the seven weeks following surgery, as I was recuperating, I continued this course. I saw the need for my community project, which I call Lightworkers Connect a Respite Resource Community Room. My original idea was to create this for healthcare workers and those on the front lines of criminal justice and public administration. This is essentially the demographic of students I provide enrollment support to in graduate programs in my current work at Walden University.

Service is my passion. Before I became a New Student Enrollment Specialist, a job I've held for 14 years, my previous career was in Social Service. I was previously an Outpatient Therapist Intern working in foster care, a Social Worker/Service Coordinator for families with children who lived with mental retardation and autism. I was also a Floor time Behavioral Specialist supporting families with children on the Autism Spectrum. I was not able to continue paying my rent without having another job, and on weekends I was a receptionist at a real estate agency, and at night I was a marketing recruiter for product testing. Full time plus two part-time jobs were too stressful to sacrifice and make ends meet.

Back then, I knew going at a frenetic pace with ongoing compassion fatigue. I surrendered and knew I had to have just one place of employment. So I resigned from all the places of employment and took the time to develop myself and started attending Professional Women Toastmasters, where I found public speaking and became a Competent Communicator and Competent Leader. I connected to a Human Resource Manager, which led me to my current position, which uses my prior education every day when I counsel graduate students' concerns and offer enrollment to programs that led to healthcare workers, police officers, probation officers, prison wardens or aspiring federal agents, attorneys and public administrators to masters degrees, to help students and their families realize their educational goals and further enhance their finances that often lead to promotions or increase their marketability in the workforce. These essential frontline workers are my graduate students, and I love to support them as a New Student Enrollment Specialist.

This was still being of service but now in higher education. My hobby job is my community project. I have uncovered within myself that I am a dynamic connector. My passion project is to have a resource page available 24/7 to bring light to the darkness in these times. Without it, burnout would continue unabated. By creating a resource respite page connecting to all the lightworkers (my community has healthcare providers, self-care professionals, wellness centers, coaching/mentoring, meditation to non-profits seeking to eradicate hate crimes, drumming circle facilitators, sound bath meditation, Project Pollyanna (www.projectpollyanna.com) founded by Dr. Heather Frederick, Ph.D.—sharing instructions on space clearing, cutting cords, aromatherapy, polyvagal recalibration, Ravi Pritnam Moments of Calm, Life Coaching and Licensed Therapist; all of whom I can refer these resources that I have known personally or recommend). My contact email is below if you would like to learn more.

These past seven weeks off work have been so very ordinary. The majority of my time was reverting to a child-like state to sleep, eat and go to the bathroom. I have learned to use my body again and rest and heal.

Going back to basic needs and rest (much-needed rest) was a restorative respite. I have short-term disability insurance and was able to take time off to rest. I practice meditation daily, the Sudarshan Kriya. "Su" means proper, "darshan" means vision and "kriya" is a purifying action through the Art of Living (www.artofliving.org). This technique helps people experience more joy and emotional freedom by eliminating toxins and bring the mind to the present moment.

This silence and rest was the respite my body and mind needed to free myself up to create my community project and say yes to writing and sharing my story in this collaborative book. I met my publisher from As You Wish Publishing, Kyra Schaefer, at that retreat in Cave Creek. At that moment for me, I learned to connect to my higher self, and there I released so much stress and past pain, received tools for radical self-care. I was onto better things for my life, creating new possibilities for my future.

I have stumbled into abundant blessings by clearing my head, making space to learn and create and restore. My body, mind and soul received this much-needed rest. I shared on a meditation retreat things I had experienced in my life and felt so very much supported. They encouraged me to share my story to help others. These experiences of self-care lead to creating my group of lightworkers. They said by sharing your story, you will make a difference.

I had shared that I never had children, and with this recent surgery, I will never be able to. I regret having an unplanned pregnancy that was terminated, and that I lived with deep regret. I now know this was a chapter and not my whole story. My life is full of love and what I got back was myself. One person shared with me that she had a wonderful aunt in her life who made such a difference who didn't have her own children, and she told me that like her aunt, I can be a symbolic mother in caring for the world. I was deeply moved and appreciated that so much. It's painful to hear, but I know it came from love. After shame, regret and tears and releasing it all, giving to God all my soul could not endure by me, I found grace. Or grace found me when I was ready to accept loving forgiveness and radical self-care by resting, filling up with gratitude and sharing my story and my resources. The divine has called me to be a dynamic connector, and I am here to be of service.

This is my chance to use my ability to connect resources to those who would welcome the practice of self-care. Living with my family and having my other brother close by has been tremendously healing. My sisters who live out of state are a text away and have been so supportive of all of the female issues. They thoughtfully made me a Godmother to their children. I don't think I could have made it through this life all on my own. All the things I thought were burdens are truly blessings. After stripping away freedom, in social isolation, I have my tribes. I can still connect to learning on social media, and I check in with my out-of-state family on text, social media and phone.

I am excited for my next experience with transformational leadership as I have just been accepted to an Introduction to Leaders program, which begins in 2021. As my life unfolds and my heart opens wider, I will be able to connect resources to people and shine a light on transformation. This is my chapter for now. I am allowing joy to come into these ordinary moments and dare myself to enjoy the light.

I am committed to being of service and living with meaning, a purpose to share my light to shine on others as they share their light and to ignite this world with kindness, love and positivity.

Bio

Aileen Balizado, MA, holds a Master's degree in Clinical Psychology with a concentration in Organizational Development from Antioch University Los Angeles. She holds a Bachelor's degree in Journalism Public Relations from Northern Arizona University. She lives in Tempe, Arizona, and is the Founder of Lightworkers Connect: A Respite Resource Community. Her email address is aileenbaliz.lightworkersconnect@gmail.com.

Thank you to my best friend Lori Moerbitz, my "non-biological sister" who I met at Northern Arizona University and Alpha Delta Pi Sorority. She also made me a Godmother to her daughter. I am so grateful for Addison, my lightworker brother, who is my constant support in his expertise in caregiving and so generously listens and holds space for me in my toughest times. Aleysha and Rachel, my warrior sisters, with no questions asked, would be there for me. For more than 30 years, I remain in contact with my faith-sharing sisters, who are beacons of light from Saint Monica's. To my soul sisters of Southern California, I zoom with and my Big Sky Meditation Community. My "Sun-shines" in Seattle, Raymond and Karen Ussery, who introduced me to Landmark Education. I am so blessed to have such loving, supportive communities to encourage me to share my light.

A Gift of Oneness
By Sarah Berkett

A sense of oneness is said to be connected to greater happiness and satisfaction with your life. Oneness with the universe is the idea that everything is interconnected and interdependent. When we experience the oneness in our lives, it is a deep feeling that we are not separate from anything that exists, but instead, we are part of a greater whole. Thus, the people we are consistently around.

Most people who have experienced oneness say they would choose to live in this state of mind if possible. Oneness is perhaps the most sought after state that a human being can ever hope to achieve, a blissful and usually fleeting sensation where we are overcome with joy and feelings of intense connection. Oneness shows us the meaning of connection in every sense of our being human. "We are here to awaken from the illusion of separateness." —Thich Nhat Hanh

You do not have to have a near-death experience or any particular belief system to experience a state of oneness. In my experience, this beautiful state of mind can occur as a spontaneous response to ordinary life events like a walk through the woods or a genuine conversation. It is merely a matter of recognizing oneness for what it is and setting your mind to it. The experience of oneness often happens when we are alone and, for me, personally happens when I am in nature. The following are my personal examples of oneness in my life, particularly in the last few years:

An experience of feeling closeness and unity to all that surrounds you.

A momentary burst of love and gratitude as you sit with cherished friends.

How I feel just gazing up at the stars and moon.

A silent awareness that strangers all around me are really my brothers and sisters.

A sense that I am in sync with the universe and breathing through the "lungs of the Earth."

Feeling in complete harmony with every being.

A sense that everything is linked and that everything we do has a deep effect on the world.

A knowing or knowledge that everything is going to be okay.

Oneness is very simple; everything is included and allowed to live according to its true nature. This is the secret that is being revealed and the opportunity that is being offered in our consciousness this very moment. We must make use of this opportunity, be prepared to give ourselves to the work that needs to be done.

The following is an excerpt from Albert Einstein, that which I found while doing research for this chapter:

A human being is a part of the whole called by the universe, a part limited in time and space. We experience ourselves, our thoughts and feelings as something separate from the rest. A kind of optical delusion of consciousness. This delusion is a kind of prison for us, restricting us to our personal desires and to affection for a few persons nearest to us. The task must be to free ourselves from the prison by widening our circle of compassion to embrace all living creatures and the whole of nature in its beauty. The true value of a human being is determined primarily by the measure and the sense in which they have obtained liberation from the self. We shall require a substantially new manner of thinking if humanity is to survive.

We can access this oneness from our powerful thoughts. Sometimes we do not notice how our thoughts can drag us down. We would not talk to our loved ones this way. So why do we always talk to ourselves in such a nasty voice? I have found that affirmations are a fantastic way to take control of what vibes you take in and let out. I would like to share with you what affirmations have helped over the last four or five ways. Pick out the one or ones that resonate with you.

My body is healthy, my mind is brilliant, my soul is tranquil.

I forgive those who have harmed me in my past and peacefully detach from them.

Creative energy surges through me and leads me to brilliant and new ideas.

Today, I abandon my old habits and take up new, more positive ones.

Everything that is happening now is happening for my ultimate good.

I wake up today with strength in my heart and clarity in my mind.

My nature is divine; I am a spiritual being.

I trust myself to deal with any problems that may arise.

I trust the universe gives me what I need at exactly the right time.

I refuse to give up because I have not tried all possible ways.

If you do not have a sacred place in your home to feel oneness, just create one. It is a beautiful way to introduce more serenity and peacefulness into your life by quieting down the mental chatter or monkey mind. No matter what we do or where we are, we tend to find ourselves surrounded by noise. The loudness of the modern world alone is hard to escape, but the constant thread of thought, the rush and the fast pace of our lives just make it that much harder to filter it all out. It is no surprise we start craving for something so simple yet so hard to obtain— silence.

If you are unsure whether you have enough space for it, do not worry. You really do not need a spare room; any place that is a bit quieter will do, for example, a little corner in your bedroom, a walk-in closet, or just a spot somewhere by a window. If you already have a place that you associate with relaxation, like a chair on which you sit in the mornings while sipping tea, this is also a great place to start. Once you decide where your sacred space will be, decorate it with meaningful things. Some people like to decorate it with crystals, Buddhas, singing bowls, books and other spiritual tools that are calming by nature, but it is totally up to you to help you with your choices. If you have personal items that carry an emotional value, that is even better. You can also fill your space with plants or inspirational things like quotes, calming music, essential oils, or the aroma of sage will help you achieve a more relaxed state. Now that you have created your own sacred space, it is time to use it. What you choose to do there is completely up to you. Some people meditate, pray or just sit there with their eyes closed for a few minutes, while others use it to paint, do something creative, or simply read a book. Anything that you deem sacred goes. I also recommend spending at least a few minutes in your sacred space every day. If you keep doing it often enough, your mind will start associating with peace, calmness, and oneness. Now that you know how sacred places help with achieving oneness go ahead and create one just for you.

Did you know that the way you begin your morning can decide how your whole day will turn out? Next, I like to share my morning ritual with you.

Practice Gratitude – If you are anything like most people nowadays, you probably reach for your phone the first thing in the morning. Instead of checking your email, social media accounts or reading news, open your eyes, roll over, grab a notebook, a journal or a piece of paper, and start writing down at least three things you are thankful for. It can be anything at all, even something as simple as having a good night's rest. Practicing gratitude on a daily basis teaches us to be more positive overall and can improve our mental well-being in numerous ways.

Stretch – Now that you worked on your mind a little bit, it is time to wake your body up. Physical exercise is a great way to kick-start your energy levels. If a high-intensity cardio workout is your thing, go for it. That's even better. But for most of us, simple stretching is something more achievable yet still highly beneficial. Simply sit up in bed, raise your arms overhead and stretch them out. After you make your way out of bed, do a few more energizing stretches to get that blood flowing.

Wake Up Your Senses – Now, this is the fun part. Pick one of your five senses and treat yourself accordingly. Play your favorite song, burn some incense or essential oils, have a little snack, give yourself a mini massage, do whatever comes to your mind to spoil either your sight, hearing, smell, taste, or touch. Just make sure to pick one thing, do not do everything all at once. Give your body and senses the love and attention they deserve and instantly raise your spirits.

Think of a Goal – I find that when I write down my goals for the day, it makes me more likely to fulfill them. It will make you feel more productive and ready to take on the day also. Even if it is only one thing that you want to achieve today, write it down. Do not forget to cross it out after it is done. That can be the most satisfying part.

Embrace Nature – regardless of where you live, taking the time to enjoy a bit of nature can help establish a positive outlook and a deeper relationship with Mother Earth. Not to mention that it is incredibly relaxing. Walk around your yard or your block, or just simply drink a cup of tea on the balcony while enjoying the morning view. I promise that you will feel refreshed and rejuvenated instantly.

Spend Quality Time With Your Pet – The mere thought of my beloved dog, Maddie, makes me tingle all over. Our pets do not just fill our hearts with love; they make it stronger. Here are a few more benefits of owning and spending time with your fur baby.

They keep you fit & active, whether walking or running.

Add meaning and purpose to our lives, stave off depression, and you will get sick less often.

You may also be less stressed at work and have a more active social life.

Each of us has an enormous potential to support, motivate, and inspire, yet we often turn to discouraging negative talk out of fear or simply out of habit. A positive relationship with yourself will last you a lifetime, so it is time to learn how to have a healthy dialogue with your inner self. If you are not sure where to start, take note of the dos and don'ts of healthy self-talk below.

Don't Do

It's Pointless I can do it It's taking ages I am still making progress It's useless I am enough, and I am valuable Everything sucks Good things are going to come to me I am too stressed I feel stronger with every breath I am ugly I am beautiful inside and out It does not matter what I think My voice always matters I am all alone I have people who love and respect me

Remember to always be your biggest supporter. Take time to nurture the relationship with yourself. After all, that is the one that will truly last you a lifetime. Emotions like love, appreciation and peace tend to spring up during experiences of oneness, and this is often a clue that you are entering into one of those connected states. All you have to do is savor these moments and linger with them longer to allow them to amplify.

Take note when you feel your mind and heart opening simultaneously, and do not be afraid to be over-inclusive in your personal definition or experiences of oneness. This is a territory where more is most certainly merrier. Feelings of oneness and connection are mutually expansive. The more alert you are to noticing oneness in new scenarios, the more you will experience it. And the natural, welcome result of these moments is the profound sense of true connection, oneness.

Bio

Sarah Berkett is the founder of Beamers Light, a soul-inspired temple of truth, magical awakenings and holistic teachings. She is a Professional Spiritual Teacher, Animal Intuitive, Angelic Life Coach, Reiki Master, Author and Visionary committed to bringing light and healing into this present realm. For the past 34 years, she has traveled extensively and has been trained by some of the top experts in her field and is versed in many types of healing modalities. She has served clients all over the world as both a Soul Level Animal Intuitive and Angelic Therapy Coach. Visit Sarah at www.beamerslight.com

Surprises
By Holly Bird

As I was sitting on my royal blue sectional sofa in my favorite spot, propped up looking out the window, sipping a glass of ice tea, I thought to myself, *"Another hot day."* The weather had been unbearable, even for Arizona. We had gone over hundred days at over one hundred degrees, and even the flowers in the garden, no matter how much I tended to them (watering and putting up extra shade), looked like they were struggling to survive. The edges of the leaves were turning brown with a crisp edge, and the colors of each flower were not as bold as they were when they first bloomed in the spring. Summer was here, and in the desert, that means the beauty is not as colorful and the heat is unbearable, not only for the plants but even most people, especially me.

As I look above the rim of my iced tea glass, I saw condensation that started to drop from the corner of my eye. I thought from the iced tea, but it was not on the glass, it was on the window: rain, could it be rain? Excitement coursed through my body as I could see more drops tapping at the window, pushing the dust that had laid on the window from the dry, dusty summer to the bottom of the sill and to my *surprise*, it was finally raining, and not even the weatherman had predicted it. As I watched it rain harder, my thoughts started to go through the *surprises* in my life, some wonderful and others not so much. I told myself quietly, "Stay positive and grateful," a mantra that I probably say a hundred times a day to myself.

As the rain became a little heavier, my thoughts went to my grandchildren and how much they love to play in the rain, and just as I began to smile, I heard a voice from the hallway: "Grandma, it's raining. Can I go out and play?" A smile came across my face, and I said, "Of course, let's go!" As he ran to the back door, I got off the sofa and went to follow him. Sometimes I felt like a little puppy following him around, watching him with awe and love and feeling blessed to be living with him every day, as we live in a multigenerational home by choice, which was another *surprise* in my life. I never thought that I would be living with my daughter, her boyfriend and my grandson by choice, and as I watched the smile on my grandson's face, it glowed, and my first thought was "grandmas little angel." I was truly blessed, and he was definitely one of my earth angels who helped me get through every day since he was born.

As my thoughts continued to wander, the one thought, Angels, seem to always take me back to my childhood and the connection I have always felt, even at a very young age, to our Heavenly Father and the gift of his Angels, I could see and feel them, and when I would try to share this with others, I could hear the laughter and disbelief from family and friends, as I could hear them say she has always been such a "storyteller" with a wild imagination, and even though I was sad and frustrated that no one believed I could feel the love and strength from my Angels to keep believing, that they would be with me forever.

As I got older, in my early teens, I learned that it just better to keep my gift to myself instead of sharing it because when I did share, the feeling of rejection and being called a liar, even though I knew that most people who were in my circle of family and friends believed in God, they did not believe that I could have a connection and feel the guidance that was a gift, not only for me but for anyone who was open and willing to believe to receive these amazing messages.

As I got into adulthood, I realized that I was losing my connection, not because it wasn't there, but because I wasn't focused on it. My life and family were always moving at a fast pace. I had forgotten to slow down and feel the connection and the gratitude I had for it.

I had been married, divorced, and a single parent and the life experiences that come with each was always a *surprise*. I never knew what to accept, but in my early forties, I met a man who would change my life forever. We would fall in love, a love I had never felt before, and raise a blended family that was filled with fun, laughter, and a faith that I had yearned for most of my life. He believed in me and my gifts, which opened my heart to my gift, and the Angels once again sang and guided me through my days. I was blessed.

Seventeen years later, I found myself writing a book, *Shaken Dreams: A Journey from Wife to Caregiver,* my story of how our lives would be changed forever by *surprises* that we never expected, health problems, family and the Angels that help support me through situations that I never could have gotten through by myself.

Writing this book was a way to share with others the lessons I learned about being a wife, juggling health problems not only mine but those of the man I loved more than life itself. As tears poured down my face for six straight weeks, I took my journals out and relived every moment and wrote, knowing in my heart, I was going to help so many people. There are hundreds of thousands of people who become caregivers to those they love, and I was hoping to help them all!

One of the harder *surprises* in my life, even though *Shaken Dreams* had made the best-seller lists in five categories, not many books sold in some of the categories. I only had to sell two or three books to make it to number one. My publisher was thrilled, and I was grateful, but I could see the number of books that had sold, and the eBooks were a little better, but the pages read never matched the books that I gave away for free, in the hope of helping others. Not only was I surprised because of the sales but surprised by my feeling of failure because I knew in my heart if I only helped one person, I would be grateful, and I was, but when we put our heart and soul into something, it is hard to accept that it wasn't as successful as I hoped.

Two years later, as I am sitting watching the joy on my grandson's face dancing in the rain, I knew that I had been blessed when I received a letter in the mail from a reader of my book, thanking me for sharing a wonderful love story and that she needed it so desperately because it gave her to insight to get through her journey, and she was able to open her heart and let the angels help her. So, I knew that no matter how disappointed I felt, that even when I am gone, my word will always be there for anyone who might need guidance through their journey.

Understand who you are and live authentically, just being you. All those concerns you have about how you look, act, or what people think doesn't matter. When you are truly yourself, you will attract the people who will appreciate you for who you really are. And, your inner and outer worlds will align, reducing stress and bringing more peace into your life. The steps are not always easy, but when you follow them, you can find oneness with God that can change your life forever.

Let your heart guide you: Your inner spirit speaks through your heart. God does too. So, use your brain as a tool to gather information, but listen to the guidance of your heart in the end.

Practice kindness and compassion: When you live a loving life, you feel surrounded by love. And, you will be making a difference in the world, whether you feel it or not. Being kind-hearted will enhance the well-being of everyone in your life, including you.

Let go of the drama and embrace peace: Don't let drama and discord take up space in your life. Limit yourself to exposure to what could be unnecessarily upsetting and focus on what is peaceful, useful, and warms your heart. Understand that there are things that you can't control, and you must let go. You will feel much better when you do.

Live simply: Don't let the things you own, your schedule, or people suffocate you. Focus your attention on what you find useful, beautiful, or meaningful and let the rest go.

Creating a sanctuary in both your heart and home will help you feel better and live with more understanding and grace.

Spend time in nature: God can be felt in nature. You don't have to be a hiker or a gardener to connect with it. The wonders of nature can be found almost anywhere, and at any time, even in a weed growing through a crack in a sidewalk. Take time to notice the beautiful natural world around you. Appreciate it, breathe it in, or take a picture to preserve the memory.

Live the truth: Living your truth includes always being honest and doing what you say you will. Dishonesty and broken agreements damage relationships and destroy trust, even if they are with you. Speaking and living the truth is one of the most empowering things you can do.

Embrace daily practices: Creating a framework for your days can improve your mood, focus, and connection to your heart. Morning practices might include journaling, reading something uplifting, exercise, meditation, or setting intentions for the day. You may want to consider a gratitude practice, relaxation, reading, praying, or something that helps you sleep well at night.

Take care of yourself: To live, you need to take care of your body. Your mind and spirit need support, too. Without self-care, your life becomes limited, but with it, your possibilities are endless.

Live in the present moment: Focusing on your present moment limits space in your mind for worrying about the future or feeling bad about the past. Too many of us live in our heads most of the time and don't notice the small moments of our days passing us by. You will be more effective and feel more grounded when you pay attention to what is happening right now.

Love yourself and learn to forgive the things and people who keep your heart heavy by finding something to be grateful for in every situation, including situations that you never thought you could find something to be grateful for. Death, deceit, and loss, such as the people who help support you through the situation. Maybe the person you lost was in so much pain, and now they are sitting with God in Heaven. I lost a child, and the one thing I found to focus on was the compassion and support of the nurses and doctors who helped me through. Yes, it was painful and even to this day brings tears to my eyes, but even though I do not know why it happened, I have to have faith that God is with my child and the best Father that he could ever have.

If you can find a way to think and feel this way, it will always help you stay positive and open to the love and blessing sent to us by our Heavenly Father every day. God bless you and your family.

Bio

Holly Bird is an internationally bestselling author of the book *Shaken Dreams: A Journey from Wife to Caregiver*, co-author of *When Angels Speak, 52 Weeks of Gratitude Journal, Kindness Crusader*. Holly is a mentor and certified Life Coach with a focus on aging health education and family. She shares her wealth of life experiences, everything from spiritual and family mentoring, marriage, gardening, cooking, traveling, and her favorite, being a grandma, on her blog.

Connect with Holly
http://www.Hollysbirdnest.com
HollyBird@hollysbirdnest.com
Facebook @hollysbirdnest
Facebook @loveyourangels
Twitter @HOLLYJBIRD

My Stroke of Insight
By Anna Carlin

T he night of the stroke, I dreamed I was in a long, dark tunnel. Cloudy gray fog swirled around me, and it thickened until it was all I could see. I woke up with a feeling of indescribable dread.

I was twenty. I was home from college, visiting my parents. When I woke up in the early hours of the morning, my right arm was asleep. I sat up and shook it. As I sat up, the numbness spread through my entire body. Even my face went numb. Even my tongue.

Probably a panic attack, I thought. Probably just stress. I had never had a panic attack before, but I'd read about them. I decided to Google it. I pulled out my laptop and tried to turn it on, but I couldn't find the button. This was very strange. I'd used that laptop a hundred times. Why couldn't I find the button? Unnerved, I got out of bed and started to my younger sister's room. My right leg was dead weight. I stumbled into her room and woke her up.

"How do you turn it on?" I asked her, holding out the laptop.

She raised her head off her pillow and squinted through the darkness at me. "Huh?"

I held out the laptop. "I can't turn it on."

"What's your problem?" she said, scrunching up her face. She pressed the "on" button and pulled the blankets back over her head.

I staggered back into my room. My right leg still wasn't cooperating. Step, drag. Step, drag. I sat down on my bed and started to type on the keyboard.

I stared down at the blinking search engine. I had forgotten how to spell "numbness." It starts with an "n," right? The letters on my keyboard had all disappeared, replaced with squiggly lines.

Something is seriously wrong with me, I realized. This is very bad.

I changed into an old gray sweatshirt and jeans. As I was getting dressed, I felt a stabbing pain on one side of my head. The pain squeezed my brain. It released, then squeezed again. I fumbled with the clothes as I put them on; the fabric kept turning to liquid between my fingers.

I went out into the hallway. Holding tightly onto the banister, I made my way downstairs. The stairs seemed to tilt as I walked down them. Everything was dark around the edges. The kitchen was filled with gray light. It was the start of the day. My mother was already downstairs, having a cup of coffee. She looked at me. "Are you okay?" she asked. The room shimmered behind her. Everything was shrinking and growing. The walls looked like they were moving.

I shook my head. Suddenly I couldn't remember the right order of words. I decided to try to speak anyway. "Feel good don't," was how it came out. The words sounded strange to me, it sounded like I was speaking Martian.

She drove me to the hospital.

I didn't have insurance, and so it took four days for me to get care, but that's another story in itself. No one would see me. While I didn't have access to treatment, my symptoms steadily worsened. Finally, a very kind doctor agreed to see me without insurance, and I was admitted to the hospital. The hospital stay was largely a blur. Doctors and nurses came and went, shaking their heads. They all had bad news. I heard two nurses talking to each other. "What a shame. A stroke. She's only twenty," they said.

Various relatives came and sat with me and held my hand, my dad and my sister and my aunt and cousins. My grandparents flew in from Pennsylvania. My hospital room was very crowded. Their visits were a bright spot, and they spent a lot of time laughing and joking with me and cheering me up. My cousins blew up a rubber glove like a balloon and bounced it around the room. The hospital put a yellow bracelet on my wrist that read, "Fall Risk." We all had a pretty good chuckle at the bracelet, as I've always been known to be clumsy. "Maybe when the hospital lets you go, you should keep the bracelet on," my dad joked.

I had damage to my left parietal, occipital, and temporal lobes. My symptoms were too numerous to list. It was sometimes hard to walk or talk. I didn't recognize the written word. I had lost a lot of vision. One side of my face drooped. I forgot that birds laid eggs. I didn't know what a hot dog or a rollercoaster was. I didn't remember what a key was or that it was to open a door. Someone showed me a picture of a snowman, and I had no idea what it was.

I was rarely alone, but when I was, I discovered that I no longer had an inner monologue. I was inside a silent mind. It was like someone had taken a remote control and pushed the "mute" button.

I was not experiencing the world around me through the screen of labels. Thoughts, concepts, boundaries dissolved. There was no difference between you or me. I experienced everything as being literally one.

When my mind stopped making noise, a space opened up within me. I felt myself being pulled into a void. It seemed that the void was inside rather than outside myself. I experienced it as a great emptiness, a vibrant nothingness.

I felt like I could vanish forever. I am aware that we are supposed to find this depressing, the idea of nonexistence, of turning to nothingness. There is a terror of nothing. But it seemed to me that nothingness is the fundamental reality. Nothing is more real than nothing. I noticed the gaps, the spaces between things, the silence between and beneath sounds. The emptiness seemed to have its own presence, similar to the way in which an artist paints the negative space first when creating a work of art. Underneath the contrast of existence and nonexistence, I sensed an underlying unity.

I've heard about other people who have had the same experience as me and who describe it in these terms. It's said that brain injuries to the temporal lobes sometimes trigger mystical experiences and open a "door of perception" in the brain. I've also read articles and think pieces that claim that the brain scans of praying nuns look different in an MRI machine. If this is true, I don't find it surprising; these stories strike me as valid.

It took about a year or two to recover. I was lucky, and I had good doctors.

The recovery period was a strange time. The mind is a filter, and without its constructs, reality looks messy, rather like a child's chaotic scribbling. Nothing was stable. Opposites were inseparable. Was that person's shirt black, or was it white? Is that object small enough to fit in the palm of my hand, or is it bigger than my body? Space and solid form were one, and I didn't know where the edges of the solids were. Things kept shrinking and growing. I had "Alice in Wonderland Syndrome." One time I was taking a bath, and the bathtub grew to the size of the room. I became very worried. How am I going to get out of this bathtub? I wondered. Luckily, it shrank back down again, and I was able to climb out.

I didn't always know where I ended and the world around me began. One morning I was enjoying breakfast when out of nowhere, a strange hand brought a glass of orange juice to my face. I jumped, and it was several moments before I realized it was my hand.

I had several out-of-body experiences. Usually, I was floating above everything or in a tunnel. The first time, I tipped onto my back and slid through a dark tunnel with rainbow lights. I felt heat up my spine, and the heat was shooting out of my hands and feet and out of the top of my head.

Without mentally labeling, I perceived the "suchness" of all things. I remember the first time after the stroke that I saw Van Gogh's painting of a green chair. I was taken aback because he had come very close to capturing the "isness" that I perceived emanating from objects. I became convinced that he surely must have seen it too. I do not wish to romanticize mental illness, but I thought perhaps sometimes the gifted, talented, and the mentally ill can perceive things that most of us cannot while operating in our "right mind" or in our ordinary states of consciousness.

The illness was difficult and painful. But there was a space around the pain. An inner stillness that goes deeper than form and which is vibrantly alive. In this stillness, I felt the oneness of myself with all things. I became deeply aware of the present moment. I didn't know what the future entailed, and so I couldn't project myself very far into it. In this field of presence, much of the structure of my mind-made identity dissolved. I was no longer identified with form but with the awareness behind it. There was grace there, hiding behind the illusions as they fell away.

I try not to get overly sentimental about the need for love and a new consciousness. But there is another way of thinking that isn't linear, a way of perceiving in patterns, images, whole situations. Psychologists call it Gestalt. I learned that when we lay aside the conventional and really just look at things, even the insignificant becomes amazing. Just an ordinary pebble, a blade of grass. These things are more than the sum of their parts. There is beauty in the ordinary, in the nothing special. There is sacredness in the everyday.

The stroke was a taste of my own mortality. I guess everyone gets that once in a while. We are all impermanent. Since my recovery, I don't get spontaneous mystical experiences much anymore, but I have to work at them. I meditate, not religiously, at 5 a.m., the way some people make a practice of and swear by, but occasionally, it works for me.

There is a saying in Zen: "Before enlightenment, chop wood, carry water. After enlightenment, chop wood, carry water." I think this is how we have to go about things, to remember the special in the ordinary, the sacred in the mundane. All the little things make up most of our lives. We can use these little things as an aid to go within. In little tasks that don't require much attention, we can use that spare attention to move into a state of presence and go deeper.

A shift in awareness can happen very easily, and it doesn't matter how long it lasts, only that it arises. There's a tendency to want to attach superhuman qualities to altered states of consciousness, and I often fall into this trap myself. I try to remember that it's just a natural state that we all can step into at any time. The moment we pay attention to the gap in our thoughts, a space opens up. I learned a trick to silence the mind at will. Simply ask yourself: "I wonder what my next thought will be?" Then wait and watch for it, the way a cat watches a mousehole.

As the beloved teacher, Ram Dass once said, "Start with your mind. Watch your mind." It can be done by meditating, by reading holy books, or just by becoming aware of the awareness. We know when we have entered that state because we no longer need to ask the question.

I'll end with a Zen story because I am partial to those. A monk asked the master to define Zen. The master took a piece of paper and wrote down one word: "Attention." The monk read it, frowned, and asked the master to elaborate. So the master wrote again, and handed the paper back. "Attention."

Bio

Anna Carlin lives in Texas with her partner and their fur babies. She enjoys painting, drawing, sculpting, reading, swimming, and Broadway musicals. Anna can be reached at AnnaCarlin89@aol.com.

Defining Moments
By Rose Bourassa

It is said the adult you have become is defined by moments in your childhood.

My parents fostered children when I was young. It was not uncommon to come home from school and find a new baby in the house. Every child who entered our doors was named, baptized and loved beyond belief. One little boy, in particular, gave us so much love in return. Donald arrived on my ninth birthday. I thought he was my present, my very own baby. While mom was changing a diaper, Donald latched on to my finger with his tiny hand.

"Mom—why does Donald have 2 thumbs?"

"Everybody has two thumbs," she answered. "Mom—look—Donald has two thumbs on one hand."

Most of the babies stayed with us for 2–3 months. Donald stayed with us for just over 18 months. Back in the '60s, that little extra thumb defined him as a "special needs" child, so he was unfortunately hard to place in a forever home.

Growing up, I vividly remember those late summer thunderstorms. I recall my dad sitting on the front porch watching the rain fall. Sometimes I would sit with him. He taught me how to watch the clouds as they moved to know when lightning would strike. We would count the seconds between the strike and the thunder to know how far away the storm center was. I loved sitting there with him. Just watching. Just listening. Just being in a shared moment with him. It was our special time together.

Summer turned to winter, and Donald still had not been placed in a forever home. Donald was about 18 months younger than my little brother. They were becoming great playmates. My parents recognized that Donald would be a great addition to our family. They decided to file papers to adopt him. He was almost two when my parents learned they would not be adopting Donald. A doctor and his wife wanted to adopt him. They were perfect for our special child. It broke our hearts to have to let him go, but the adoption agency felt a doctor was a much better fit than a seamstress and baker for a righty with two thumbs.

Donald was the last baby my parents ever fostered. They just couldn't go through that hurt again. Dad spent lots of rainy days on the porch after that. Somehow, it couldn't fix the broken heart.

For several years after Donald left, Dad and I continued sitting on the porch watching the rain. Sometimes my dad would have a most serious look on his face. I would ask if something was wrong. "Not for you to worry about," he'd say. "Besides, the rain is going to wash away all the problems in the world, and everything will be new again. The plants will grow, and so will you! And after the storm has passed, the world will be refreshed. New again. You will see everything in a different light."

My dad was famous for telling me, "When you have a problem, think about it carefully, then turn it over and think about it from the other side." Wise words I follow to this day.

Resolving the problems of the world from the front porch during a rainstorm became a treat for me. I never knew what issue we would resolve, but I always knew we would.

I only remember seeing my father cry one time in my life. When I was in my early teens, my father was diagnosed with lung cancer. Before he left for the hospital for surgery, he held each one of us tightly and cried as though he knew he wouldn't be back. But he did come home again. All fresh and new.

Looking back now on that first rainstorm after Donald got his forever home, I recall my dad standing in the rain. At the time, I thought he was just crazy, but now I believe he stood there in the downpour, so none of us would see him crying. This was his way of mourning the son he loved but didn't get to keep.

All my life, I have jumped from one career to another. I couldn't make up my mind what I wanted to be when I grew up—but I always knew whatever it was would include a husband, a house with a white picket fence, a couple of kids and a dog. And I knew that one of those kids would be adopted.

Eventually, I did grow up, marry, buy a house and get a dog. All that was missing were the kids.

I had always envisioned having one baby and adopting one of the opposite sex. After a few years, we decided we would try adopting first (you know those stories about how the minute you adopt, you get pregnant?) It was a long process, too long for me. I was ready for them to hand me a baby the minute I walked through the door. Through the process, when it rained, I would fall back to that front porch with my dad and process all the information and resolve my problems.

I would think things through from many different sides. Sometimes I would go outside in the rain and let it cleanse my soul of all the impatience I had waiting for a baby. Then we got the call.

We had been selected to be parents. Party time! Ten days later, we brought home the most perfect little boy in the world. Ten fingers, ten toes, cute as could be. Perfect in every way.

My parents were in Chicago when we brought our son home. I couldn't wait for them to get back to meet the little guy. It was heaven on earth. And Dad was the grandpa who had to teach him razzberries only to have his grandson give them back to him one day while he was trying to scold him. He was a wonderful grandpa. Sadly, we lost him when our son was three.

Four years later, we submitted papers to adopt a second baby. This child must have been conceived the day we filed. Nine months from submission to bringing her home.

She was born 6 weeks early, a whopping 4 lbs 13 oz. and had a bilateral cleft palate.

There are varying degrees of cleft. Hers was the worst form. We had to understand her physical requirements and know that we would be able to care for her in the way she would need.

We talked to doctors, dentists, read books on how to care for a child with her form of a bilateral cleft pallet. It turned out to be a piece of cake. Our adoption agency eventually asked us to answer the big question: "Are you willing to adopt this child?"

Yes! Three little letters and she was all ours. Our teeny, tiny "special needs" baby, and we couldn't be more happy or blessed.

We had no clue as to what to expect. We didn't know she would not sleep through the night till she was four. Or that she would need to eat every two hours (something she does to this day!). Or that after her first corrective surgery, her big brother would begin to refer to her as an alien monkey. (Eventually, he dropped the alien and just called her monkey.)

We had no idea that when your child has casts on her arms after surgery, she can relocate your jaw with one smooth swing. Or that she would develop night terrors, and the only person who could calm her was Dad. Night terrors—so much to learn on that front. We asked the doctor about how to deal with it, and she told us, "Wine." For the baby? We're not giving our little one wine! "No," she said. "Not for the baby—for you!"

The night terrors would eventually stop. But until they did, there were days when I wondered if there was enough wine in the world to get through them. I prayed for a night when this child would sleep longer than forty minutes!

The biggest bridge we had to cross with this child was that she was a girl. Our son had told everyone at school he was going to be a big brother—to another boy. It took some creative questioning to figure out why we could only adopt another boy. We learned it all came down to a name. We had discussed names for boys, but not for girls! So we sat down and spent an entire afternoon going through the names of girls he went to school with before we finally agreed on a little girl's name. Good thing we did. She entered our lives a few weeks later. Two days after she came home, her big brother took her to school for show and tell.

Yep—he was proud of his little sister. Showed her off everywhere we went. Not only was he the big brother, he was also a teacher. He taught the kids at school about cleft palate and how it was okay to be different. You could be different and still be a person who needs love and gives love in return. A person who is just as normal as you or me. Our little special needs girl was truly special, not because of her medical disability, but because she helped educate so many young people about physical deformities. All the kids in school followed her progress. Everyone at our church was in love with her. We couldn't go anywhere without her. She was changing perceptions with her cute little smile and her big heart.

She had the greatest doctor in the world tending to her cleft palate. No white coat for her. Sometimes she would sit on the floor with her and play a game to make her laugh so she could sneak a peek inside her mouth. We also had a whole team of specialists who looked after everything else: speech, hearing, teeth, genetics and anything else you can think of. Each of them with a very special love for children.

We saw that team once a year for 21 years. In between, we had the occasional corrective surgery scheduled just at the right time in her life. And two sets of braces! Through it all, she had a loving family who supported her all along the way. We had an extended family that was always there for her. Her circle of friends were true friends and remain so to this day. This circle never saw her as different. They only saw the sweetest, cutest little girl on the planet.

Through it all, she has grown into a beautiful young woman. A humorous individual. A person who knows the value of love. A young woman who ends every conversation with her mom with an "I love you." A young woman who has had a few defining moments of her own in her life that will help her on her path.

Sometimes in the winter, when it rains, I sneak out to the patio and watch the rainfall. I ponder all the problems in my life and contemplate how to resolve them. Since Dad's been gone, it's lonely outside in the rain, but I still hear his words: "Think about it carefully and then turn it over and think about it from the other side."

Dad used to say that the rain washed everything new again. He loved the smell of the world after it rained. It brought such love, peace and hope for the freshly washed world. I wonder if he knew that the way it smells after a rain is called *Petrichor*. It probably wouldn't have mattered to him. He would say it smelled like love.

Bio

Rose Bourassa is a retired procurement specialist and an international bestselling author for her contribution to the book, *The Grateful Soul*. She is currently preparing for a second career as an evidential medium and proprietor of her own spiritual center. She is a wife, mother, grandmother, student, teacher and volunteer. To keep sharp, she strives to learn something new every day, hopefully, something to help keep up with grandkids. Even when they have to dumb it down! You can reach Rose via email at Remnick@aol.com.

The Impossible is Not So Impossible
By Patricia Burlison

As I look at the car loaded up with boxes, I remember the struggle it took to get here. My son, Sabastian, was born on July 19, 2000, at 27 ½ weeks gestation. I didn't know day to day if my little miracle was going to survive. After all, his twin sister didn't. His doctor at St Joseph's Hospital in Phoenix, AZ, gave him an 82% chance of survival and a 100% survival rate if he surpassed thirty days.

Thirty days! I cried and prayed nonstop for thirty days. His first birthday party was on August 17, 2000. He survived 30 days! At that point, I knew the Lord had special plans for him. I celebrate every milestone. From holding his body temperature to breathing on his own to graduating kindergarten and high school, to earning his first karate belt, to winning swim meets, to attending his first political rally, to getting into the only university he applied to when all the school administrators told us it wasn't possible, to everything in between.

Sabastian was a typical little boy. He mostly played inside with army men. He had thousands of them, and I kept buying them. Don't ask me why. He just loved them. He told me he wanted to join the military. I chuckled and said, "Okay." After all, we come from a military family. I thought he would grow out of it after one of my mom's best friends told me he would. I didn't think much of it after that.

Sabastian always struggled in school. I thought if he repeated kindergarten, he would become more mature and would be able to keep up with the other students. Sitting with his team of educators, it was suggested to label him with having a learning disability. All I could do at the time was cry and explain to them that I didn't want to label my son. But, I also didn't want him to fall through the cracks. I knew that if I didn't keep a close eye on him and his studies, he would get lost in the system. I was not going to let that happen. I left that meeting with swollen eyes and an Individual Education Plan (IEP). My son was moving on to first grade.

I attended every Back-to-School, Parent-Teacher Conference, and IEP meeting there was. I was on top of his education, or so I thought. We had some issues, though. He had a hard time focusing and staying on task. He was self-conscious because he wore glasses, and the kids on the bus would make fun of him, and he had low self-esteem because he wasn't great at sports. One kid, in particular, would bully him daily because of his lack of sporting abilities. Being self-conscious, having low self-esteem and being bullied by the same kid daily can be a deadly combination.

I made sure to always lift him up. We attended church and lived a well-balanced life at home. I would help him with his homework whenever he needed it, and I made sure to always be present. I went out of my way to praise him and remind him how smart he was and how he'll accomplish all his goals as long as he stayed on the right path.

He was one of the more quiet students and was always respectful to his teachers. We both took pride in his behavior at school. Trouble was looming, and I didn't even realize it. His IEP expired during the middle of his sixth-grade year. He was doing so well I had nothing to worry about. That all changed when he was promoted to seventh grade.

Throughout elementary school, Sabastian was still talking about going into the military. I kept thinking he was going to grow out of that silly idea. My only child wants to join the military! What do I do to talk him out of it? I told him that he was too smart to go in straight from high school, so if he wanted my blessing, he would have to go to college and earn at least a four-year degree. He agreed! From that point on, we knew he would attend a university. We were both delighted with our compromise.

Sabastian was failing nearly every course in seventh grade. I couldn't understand what was happening. I was furious with him. By that time, I was working on my Master's degree. My student saw me work hard to accomplish goals. He knew I loved school, and I knew he loved school. What was happening? We ended up meeting with another team of educators. This time was different, and I mean very different. For the first time, I saw red while talking to administrators!

At the start of the meeting, the school psychologist asked me if Sabastian had ADHD and what medication he was on. I was insulted! How dare someone who doesn't know my child think that he has a medical condition. I advised him Sabastian isn't ADHD and he doesn't take any medications. He then suggested I take him to his primary care physician and gave us a test to complete with hundreds of questions on it. I thought the school psychologist was a quack!

During the same meeting, the school counselor told Sabastian and me that he would never attend a university. She said he didn't have what it took to be a successful university student and that community college would be best for him. Again, I cried and told her that community college isn't in the plan and that he will attend a university. We went back and forth, and through my tears, I told her that she should be ashamed of herself for saying what she's saying in front of a child who already has low self-esteem.

I took Sabastian to his primary care physician, and sure enough, he was diagnosed with ADHD and was prescribed Vyvanse. Wow! What a difference. He went from failing to the honor roll! He sailed through middle school. I was even fortunate enough to become the PTSA's president. I was there every step of the way, building up his self-esteem! Life was good! God was good! Then came high school.

Sabastian loved high school. He was in the AFJROTC and kept his eye on his dream of joining the military. I did have to remind him every so often of our deal. He breezed through his freshman and sophomore years. He even won the Tuskegee Airmen Incorporated AFJROTC Cadet Award and was inducted into the Kitty Hawk Air Society. Both are prestigious national awards. Life couldn't be any greater!

Then he got to his junior year. He didn't apply himself as he should have, and the fights started. They got louder and more frequent. I couldn't understand how my national award-winning student could be messing up so badly. I asked myself if he was drinking alcohol, trying illegal drugs, or participating in sexual activities. I went through his social media accounts, his phone, his backpack, and his room. Nothing was out of the norm. He was being a teenager and was losing his focus. I didn't know what to do except continue lifting him up with praise and being present.

His senior year was the toughest. He knew what grades he needed to earn to be able to get into an Arizona university. He earned his first "D" during his first semester. I went through the roof. I was so angry and so hurt. I actually took it personally because I worked so hard to make sure he was going to be able to accomplish his dreams. I would yell and cry and ask him how he expected to get into the university with those grades. He told me that he would improve his studies. All I could do was believe him.

During winter break, his doctor and I decided to wean him off his Vyvanse. If he wanted to join the military, he had to be drug-free for two years. So, he went into his last semester of high school with no medication, all the while holding my breath that everything will work out. Sabastian still had his IEP, and every year since second grade, we would meet with his teachers and administrators to set up new goals and to measure his progress. It was during the last meeting in November 2017 that changed everything.

According to the administrators at Shadow Mountain High School, he was not on track to attend an in-state university because he has an IEP. He will graduate high school, but he will have deficits in science and in math and not have fine art on his final transcript. I was furious! I was so angry I screamed at everyone in that room except for his teachers. No one knows your child and your child's abilities except you! If you take anything from this essay, remember that.

His teachers knew he had potential and that he was smart, but the administrators did not. Sabastian ended up having to go to night school and get extra tutoring. In one quarter, he went to night school Monday through Thursday to make up two math classes and one fine art. After some time, I discovered he was failing math. His teacher didn't even notify me. The lack of respect that is shown to parents is unbelievable. No one cares about your children the way you do. I stormed into their office and asked for a meeting right there right now. I spoke with the administrator who was in charge, and for the first time in my life, I slammed my hand down on the table so hard I actually hurt myself while screaming at her. I suggested she retire if she wasn't going to make sure the kids at her school were successful. I explained to her that Sabastian needed these classes to be able to attend an in-state university. I tutored my child in classes I took years ago, but I did the best I could, and he ended up with a "C" in both of those math classes.

His last quarter was eventful as well. He didn't need night school, but he needed more tutoring than I could offer him. I signed him up for Sylvan Learning Center, and what a blessing that was. He was able to pass College Algebra with a little help from me and take the prep ACT course. The struggle continued. The tears and fights continued. Then we decided to visit Northern Arizona University for kicks-and-giggles.

Sabastian loved NAU, and he wanted to apply. He didn't want to apply to any other university except NAU. As a parent, I advised him to not put all his eggs in one basket and that he needed to have more options. Well, he didn't want more options. He wanted NAU, and that was that. He took the ACT and ended up scoring an 18, and he applied to Northern Arizona University. By the time he graduated, we still didn't have a definite answer from NAU, but we got the first approval. That's right! My child with an IEP since first grade, and all the administrators from middle school and high school telling him he would never attend an in-state university got accepted into the only school he applied to.

Currently, Sabastian is in his junior year at NAU and doing remarkably well. He made a point to request services from the Disabilities Department and is in control of his own life. He's making his dreams come true!

In writing this, I want to give hope to all the parents out there who have children struggling. You will fight and cry, but you will get through it. Remember, the impossible is not so impossible.

Bio

Patricia Burlison is a mother of twins, an International Best Selling Author, Political Activist, Student Cheerleader, and the current Chairman of Democracy of America - Maricopa County. She resides in Phoenix, Arizona and holds a Master 's Degree in Business Administration and currently works in public health. In her free time, she enjoys watching the Los Angeles Dodgers, traveling the world, and entertaining family and friends with her son, Sabastian. She invites parents or anyone who has children struggling to contact her. She can be reached at patricia.burlison@hotmail.com.

A Rainbow in the Clouds
By K.C. Cooper

As a little girl, I paid attention to the good and bad things happening around me. I was very quiet and shy and spent most of my days (while not in school) watching television shows that displayed a good moral compass in their characters, such as *The Brady Bunch*, *Good Times*, *The Facts of Life*, etc. Even though my mom always said I was a good girl, and she never had any problems with me, these shows confirmed what the small voice in my head always said. If you do wrong, you will suffer the consequences of your actions. If you lie, cheat, or steal, you will get caught (sooner or later). So you might as well do right to receive the blessings and avoid the unnecessary pain and regret that follows unethical behavior.

I also saw the repercussions of people who chose to use drugs and alcohol on a regular basis. They did not present themselves in the best way possible and often ended up in a downward spiral toward addiction. Therefore, I knew what not to do. Nevertheless, I had a very good childhood and was happy. Although I'm not perfect and have made mistakes, my character has remained intact.

By the time I became a teenager, my mom unofficially adopted a daughter. She was 14, and I was 13. She was more mature than girls our age, but still kind and humble. My mom sat us down and explained that no matter who comes around, we were never to let anyone come between us. We grew closer and closer as time went on. About two years later, we moved to a city east of Los Angeles. The community was predominately Hispanic, and we made friends easily. My sister started picking up some habits from her friends and attempted to wear bold eyeshadows, blush, and other makeup similar to theirs. When she came home from school, our mom saw her and said, "Take that war paint off your face!" She was embarrassed and immediately went to wash it off. Both of us have dark complexions, and naturally, the makeup they wore did not look the same on us, but I was not interested in wearing it.

One day my sister got upset with me because I told on her about a guy she liked. Later that night, we laid in our beds and began writing notes to each other. I apologized to her, and she forgave me. We kept passing the paper back and forth without speaking, and I confessed to her that I was tired of being a virgin. Boys at the new school were flirting with me, and I didn't know how to respond. A few days later, mama told us, "I found y'alls letter." We looked at each other horrified! We knew there were things in there that we didn't want her to know. We waited for the long talk and punishment to come, but it never did. We began to entertain the advances of a couple of boys we liked. Mama was a nurse and worked the graveyard shift. My stepfather slept like a rock, so it was fairly easy to have company over. Well, to make a long story short, I got pregnant the first time I had sex. When mama took me to the clinic, and the test came back positive, I was scared. We discussed my options, and she asked me what I wanted to do? Have the baby or get an abortion? I told her the guy was a football star with the potential of getting a scholarship, and I didn't want to mess up his future or mine. She said, "Okay," and apparently scheduled the procedure. She took me home, had me change, and whooped my butt. I understood: I did something wrong, and those were the consequences. I made peace with it and never looked back.

Now I'm going to make an attempt to fast forward to other life-changing events that followed and how I overcame them. Yet, my plan is to save as many details as possible for my memoir.

I was still a teenager when I moved from California back to Arizona. I was enrolled in the local high school and eventually met a guy that was four years older than me. He was out of school. I didn't really ask his age in the beginning. I just knew he was handsome, charismatic, and had a good sense of humor. I wasn't used to someone making me laugh so much. I gave him my number (before cell phones existed), and we spent hours at a time on the phone. Several months later, while visiting him at his house, he said, "Don't you think it's about that time?" I said, "Time for what?" He implied to have sex. I said, "I'm not really into that." He responded, "You will be by the time I'm done with you." One thing led to another, and it wasn't long before I was pregnant again. We got our own place, and he worked at one of the local gins. He gave me his paycheck every week, and we were on our way to being a happy family. *Until* one of his friends came by the house one day while he was at work and I let him know. He began to act paranoid. He was checking for footprints around the house when he came home and told me what men in town wore, what size shoes, etc. He became physically abusive, especially when he was intoxicated. I made attempts to leave him, but he said there was nowhere I could go without him finding me. He said he copied the addresses of all my relatives in California. I was 19 when I wound up in the hospital. The state picked up the charges, and he was sentenced to five years in prison. I knew I deserved to be happy, but the next guy would have to have some brothers. I had a feeling my ex wasn't done. He was a daredevil. I had to leave Arizona for a while because gossip was second nature to most of the residents in these small towns. I had a brief pity party by myself, but realized my wounds would heal, and I would be okay. The sun was gonna shine whether I wore a frown or a smile. So I chose to smile.

I enjoyed the next five years traveling back and forth to California. I dressed my daughter like a Barbie doll, with Quinceanera dresses, ruffled socks, and dress shoes. Her hair was usually braided with matching colored beads hanging from the ends. Life was good and I felt *free*. I learned more about myself, enrolled in college, and started pursuing my dreams.

By the time I entertained the thought of being in a relationship again, a younger guy was spending time at my apartment with my younger male cousin, who was living with me at the time. I noticed him watching me and kind of blushing when we spoke. When I evaluated the possibility, my first thought was that he has a lot of brothers (check). We started dating, and he was so sweet. Over time, it ended with me filing my second restraining order. I didn't share the details of the first one. Afterwards, I prayed and asked God; "Why do I keep going through this?" That still small voice said, "You're not taking enough time to get to know them before you jump into a relationship." I said, "Okay. I understand."

I shut down and made a list of everything I needed to change about myself. I listed the good things on the left side of the paper, and the dislikes on the right. I started exercising to lose the 25-30 pounds I had gained from stress eating, distanced myself from negative people, and focused on reaching my goals. I worked two jobs to pay off my car and other necessities and stayed single for two years.

Then a man I'd seen several times before started ordering pizzas. Apparently, he would call to see if I was working before placing his order. He asked me for my number a few times, and I eventually gave it to him. He was tall, dark, handsome, and always polite and respectful. He would call, and we talked once or twice a week for a whole year without going on a date. We lived about ten miles from each other, and he *never* asked me if he could come over. Our conversations went from minutes to hours. We started sharing our deepest secrets and most embarrassing moments. I could go on and on about how great this man is, but to expedite the story, we've been happily married for 26 years. We work hard, communicate, and compromise when necessary. We've experienced a few hurdles along the way, but nothing major. Our smiles are genuine, and our love is true. However, in my lifetime I have learned to keep my cup half full and allow others the opportunity to add to it.

In 2008, I started having some abnormal symptoms. I went to the doctor, and they ran tests. They called me a few days later, and I happened to be outside on my lunch break. She said, "The doctor wants to see you. Can you come in today?" I said, "Today is not a good day. I'm really busy with Paralegal appointments, etc." She said, "They found abnormal cells." I asked, "Is it okay if I come tomorrow?" She said, "Did you hear me? *You have cancer!*" I paused and said, "Okay. It'll take me about 30-45 minutes to get there." She said, "Okay. We'll see you then." I sat in my vehicle, staring straight ahead, as the objects in front of me became a blur. My eyes filled with tears, and they started falling before I could get a Kleenex. I tried to steady my voice as I called Main Control to tell them that I would not be back in today. I notified my supervisor and left. I called my husband and told him what they said, and his heart dropped. He said, "Okay. I'll meet you at home, and drive us from there." I wound up having three surgeries in four months. My outlook on life totally shifted! I was working on a job I did not like, I was not pursuing my goals of furthering my education, or becoming a writer like I wanted to be. Once I recovered and was cancer-free, divine intervention allowed me to stop working, and still be blessed with a pension.

Surviving cancer made me realize that tomorrow is not promised, and I needed to start enjoying the life I have. My husband and I have started traveling to other countries, having drinks on the beach, parasailing, swimming in caves, etc. I enjoy listening to music (meditation, jazz, or slow jams), lighting scented candles and having a glass of wine while sitting in a bubble bath. I like to read, write, dance, enjoy family time, and socialize for peace and happiness. I am the author of my fate, and so are you!

Bio

K.C. Cooper is happily married to a veteran of the U.S. Navy, has 4 children and 3 grandchildren. She retired from the Arizona Department of Corrections after 30 years of service (7 years as a Correctional Officer, and 23 years as a Legal/Resource Librarian). She currently holds a Small Business Management Certificate, is a small business owner, and plans to pursue her degree in Business Administration. She has a Bachelor's Degree in Biblical Studies and is one of the Best Selling Authors in the collaborative book: *Love Meets Life* compiled by Tara Ijai, and published by As You Wish Publishing. She is a cancer survivor and a spiritual person who seeks to fulfill her purpose in life by helping others through words, service, and life-changing opportunities. She also has a desire to help women in abusive relationships. She became an activist for social justice in 2016 and is currently studying Black History to assist in improving the conditions of urban communities. She can be reached at kcooper36@outlook.com.

Fated
By Angelique Culver

As I sit in a familiar chair, put my feet up, cover my legs with a warm blanket, and select a television channel, I am taken back to 2008.

I had just begun a new job. I was four months into my new job, to be exact. The season was preparing to transition from spring to summer.

There was nothing extraordinary or out of the usual at this time. I was 28 then, my career was moving forward, I was enjoying my life.

As I sat in that recliner for the first time, put my feet up, took calls from work, with my laptop on my personal arm table, I was ready for a fight. The nurse came by with my medication, hooked me up to my first infusion pump; my thought: 'Bring it on.'

I could do this. I could beat this. Of course, I could. I was not alone. The nurse began my first chemotherapy session, and my life was forever changed.

A month earlier, I had been diagnosed with an aggressive form of breast cancer. My world went reeling. What if I need help? What about my job? The job I had just started? Where do I go from here?

The first step, Tex-Mex and a stiff martini. Next stop, to the doctor to find out what treatment I needed. That did not go so well. The doctor treated me like a number, like every other patient he had ever seen in my shoes. But this was my life. Cookie-cutter was not going to cut it.

I can't remember if I felt afraid, but I was certainly apprehensive. It was time to tell my boss of four months that I had just been diagnosed with breast cancer.

At the time, I was an attorney for a hospital system. My boss, the general counsel. As an attorney for the legal department of a hospital, I worked closely with the general counsel, the chief medical officer, and the chief human resources officer. These three people were the key to my successful battle with breast cancer in 2008.

Upon being informed that I had been diagnosed with cancer and that I was looking for a second opinion, my boss picked up the phone then and there. We immediately called the chief medical officer. He gave me the name and contact information for the doctor that would become my surgical oncologist. I was no longer a number, just another cancer patient. I was now a person with a problem in need of solving.

Within the week, I had a treatment team I knew I could count on to save my life. My apprehension did not subside. Sure, I had a world-class treatment team. I had the full support of my boss of only four months and my chief medical officer. But fighting cancer requires time and focus.

Focus I had. Time was my worry. The first time I put my feet up in that recliner, I knew I was signing up for a year of active treatment. Chemotherapy, surgery, radiation, biological infusions. With only four months on the job, a year I did not have to take.

The next call my boss made was to the chief human resources officer. The plan, donation of Paid Time Off (PTO). The outpouring of PTO donations was amazing to live through. I didn't just have the support of my boss, my chief medical officer, and chief human resources officer; I had the support of my department and my hospital.

It was as if the building blocks of support I needed not only to fight, but to win the fight had been put in place in my life at just the right time. I had a world-class treatment team and the support of my job. I breathed a slight sigh of relief.

I still had a year of active treatment to get through. I lived in Atlanta, Georgia. My family lived in Arizona. I didn't know how I was going to do it. I lived alone. I did not know how I was going to do it. My family and friends did. My family took turns flying from Arizona to Atlanta to help me. My friends did many things, cooked meals for me to freeze and heat up later, took me to and from treatments, let me crash at their homes when I couldn't make it to my own.

That year flew by. And so did the next twelve. With the support of those around me, I had remained cancer-free for twelve years.

It was 2020. I was living in Pennsylvania. I had a new job. This time, it had been six years. I still worked for a healthcare company. I still worked with leadership. I had been seeing my medical oncologist in Pennsylvania for at least five years. Things were good. I was cancer-free.

Then I felt pain in my ribs. It didn't go away. The emergency room doctor told me it was cancer—in my lungs. When it was all said and done, I was diagnosed with metastatic breast cancer. I had cancer in my lungs, in my liver, in my brain, and in my bones. Here we were again.

I had to start over. I had to tell my boss. I had to tell my family. I had to tell my friends. I did not know what treatment was going to look like. I may as well have lived alone. I lived in Pennsylvania. My family, still in Arizona.

I was apprehensive all over again. What was I going to do? Then, I told my boss. He was more supportive than I ever could have asked. My co-workers, concerned, supportive. A friend with the same illness, cancer that doesn't go away. A family that was able to fly from Arizona to Pennsylvania to help me.

As I sat down in that recliner, put my feet up, and covered my legs with a warm blanket, I couldn't help but think this was fated. Not a fate anyone wants. Surely not a fate anyone would ever ask for. But the building blocks of support were in place before my feet went up in 2020. Just like they were in 2008. I was in another state. I was at another job. But, what stayed the same? The care, concern and compassion of those around me. I may be fated to spend my days in a recliner, with my feet up, warm blanket on my legs, hooked to an infusion pump, receiving cancer treatment. But I do so surrounded by love and warmth, one with that and those around me.

Bio

Angelique Culver, Esq. is a 16-year Healthcare Attorney, specializing in Compliance and Privacy and Security for 9 years. She is Chief Compliance Officer for Vibra Healthcare, LLC and an advocate for patients' rights. Culver is licensed to practice law in Pennsylvania and Georgia. She holds a Bachelor of Arts degree from Spelman College, a Juris Doctorate from Georgetown University Law Center, a Masters of Law in Labor and Employment from Atlanta's John Marshall Law School, and is certified in healthcare compliance. She has served as members of the bioethics committee (academic medical center); the Georgia Department of Public Health's Health Information Exchange Legal/Ethical Workgroup; former member, Board of Directors for WITF, Inc., a Central Pennsylvania public broadcasting company committed to cultural access, public education, strengthening community life through broadcasting, social media, print, and in-person events. angeliqueculver@bellsouth.net

Playing The Way to School Success
By Diana Culver, Ph.D., M.Ed.

laying the way to school success is vital to all children. Some children, primarily black, other minorities, disabled and poor children in that order are often/have been historically relegated to the school to prison pipeline. These children are often subjected to much harsher discipline than their peers for the same infractions. In rural and urban areas, children are frequently subjected to exclusionary discipline early, thus destroying their self-esteem, disenfranchising them from their childhood and making them easy prey for drug dealers and gangs. The weapon used against these children is the zero-tolerance policy designed to reduce guns in schools. This policy is twisted and abused by some administrators nationwide, and perhaps there are similar attacks on young children of color or poverty world-wide. These children must be armed with tools to counter these attacks through social-emotional mastery and a culture of supportive peers and adults.

These tools prepare them to identify and manage their emotions before they are excluded from school for being childish as early as preschool. There are fun and funny brief examples of a few solutions to help combat the above-described problem. The best way to help these children, all children, is to meet them where they are and individualize solutions for them. Play-based social-emotional learning is a positive way to help children learn to identify and express their emotions, thus decreasing the instances of negative interactions described above.

Children learn best through play (preschool to third grade); therefore, in order to teacher-proof (from those who might prejudge them), these children must be given tools early on to help them identify and manage their emotions. It is effective to introduce social-emotional play-based learning in early childhood using response to intervention (RTI). RTI is a three-tiered learning process. The first tier is the introduction of concepts, rules or ideas to the entire group. The second tier is targeted intervention, which includes teachers joining child-directed group play to help children master the concepts. The third tier is focused intervention for the child that has difficulty mastering the introduced concepts. This is accomplished through one on one play with any individual child as much as the child needs. RTI is effective with all age groups. Play-based learning assumes different forms as children grow and evolve into teens and tweens. Material can be adapted to meet cultural needs as well as meeting children who may have seen too much, experienced trauma and are street smart at an early age.

Children learning to identify and manage their emotions can be accomplished best through introducing concepts during big group time (circle time) in preschool or kindergarten. Following up in small groups and child-directed play is helpful in mastering the concepts. Play-based learning is recommended through third grade. Supportive props like feelings charts, dolls with emotions, puppets and books support the learning process. Children practice these concepts during child-directed play with their peers. Teachers assume the role of facilitator and observe and at times join play in order to reinforce learned skills or guide them toward mastering the introduced concepts. Children needing extra help grasping the concepts receive one on one time playing out and practicing learned concepts with their teachers. During play, children often correct or redirect their peers. They will intercede and ask a peer how they are feeling and encourage them to express their feeling to the other person they are upset or happy with. The importance of this practice is that children who go to kindergarten at five and are not able to identify and express their emotions panic, may have a temper tantrum out of frustration and be excluded from school.

In a play-based diverse early learning center, children are introduced to very basic feelings charts as toddlers, and their teacher helps them identify their feelings and reaffirms their feelings during playtime, meals, group time and even while toileting or diapering. The constant verbal interaction helps reinforce the validity of their feelings in the emergent social-emotional development of the toddler. Children with this foundation are well prepared for prekindergarten and eager to move on to mastering more complex feelings. One by-product of learning this with no attention paid to the complexion of their playmates and many children in attendance with siblings and cousins was the freedom from learning hate and prejudice early on. A four-year-old white girl named Julie (names changed, of course) saw a jacket and told the teacher at her other school, "that jacket belongs to my cousin." Every day the teacher looked for a little white boy to give the jacket to. They were on the playground, and Julie told her teacher," That's my cousin Kyl, it's his jacket!" pointing at a little black boy from another class. When this class moved on to elementary school, there was a child that was obese, and children on the bus were teasing her. A little boy from the same prekindergarten class told the bullies that they could not pick on his cousin. One child was white and the other black. They both were into break dancing cousins since they were toddlers. These children went all through school together and helped their cousins keep their cool and reminded each other to express their feelings in a calm manner (social-emotional competency) instead of becoming upset. Some had problems here and there. Most are responsible young adults now.

There were male teachers with all ages. The children at the center thought their male teachers were superstars, and if they saw them in public, they shouted across the store and introduced them to whoever they were with. These young men are the ultimate kid whisperers. There were three cousins that were particularly rambunctious, and their male teacher took them on shopping field trips and other life skills errands in addition to regular field trips to help expand their horizons and perhaps help them identify areas of interest for them. Their teacher took them on a shopping trip in a warehouse store (the boys were about 10 or 11). Their conversation was focused on who was fighting at school. Their teacher distracted them by repeating their conversation, substituting the word "altercation" for "fight," and told them that if they wanted to have that conversation, they had to use the word altercation instead of fight. They quickly decided it would be more fun to learn more big words for things than continue talking about fights. These boys had developed social-emotional competency in prekindergarten but were transitioning to tweens and needed some tweaking, No one knows how many altercations their new word kept them from, but as teenagers, they recounted the story to other adults and said it was difficult to have altercations because every time they thought of the word they laughed and just had to walk away. One of the young men is quite an accomplished boxer in his early 20's. He ran into his former teacher and shared that he had decided to make a career out of altercations and described his accomplishments. One of the young men has two small children who attend the same center because he wants them to have the same opportunities he had there.

There was a group of tween girls identified by their school as having difficulties with gossip and altercations at school, as were most of the girls in that age group. Their pre-kindergarten teacher volunteered to go to their school and facilitate an after-school leadership club. The girls learned conflict resolution techniques, they were trained as peer mediators and became master negotiators through practice using objects that appealed to them. Each girl got several of the same item that appeal to young girls or young people. Each girl had a different item. They were then given 15 minutes to negotiate with the other girls to get the things they really wanted. Dollar store items that come in a multi-pack were great tools for them to use to understand how much they were willing to give up to get what they wanted. This exercise in negotiation better prepared them as peer mediators. The girls also focused on some positive affirmations and responses to negative comments they encountered. One lesson was decreasing participation in gossip that ultimately led to unnecessary altercations. The response was "I don't participate in drama!" and to walk away when someone approached them with gossip. They also used, "I'm sorry you are having a bad day, I hope it gets better," when people were mean or rude to them and again to walk away. Each girl had a pocket calendar with her affirmations in the front of her calendar and recorded their success and challenges on their calendar. At Christmas time, they made drama-free zone shirts and decorated them the way they liked. Their positive inter-actions were increasing, and negative interactions were decreasing. In mid-January, one of the girls came in very indignant and proclaimed, "They are copying us; people not in our club are saying I don't participate in drama." The facilitator explained to them all that people emulating their positive behavior is what made them leaders. The indignant girl was then excited. These girls are young women now, and at least a few are young mothers. There are creative ways to apply social-emotional training on every level at every age and at every ability.

These are some examples here to help people overcome obstacles in their way. Propose that your school design an alternative to exclusionary discipline even in substance issues. People have the power to help dismantle the school-to-prison pipeline. Contact your local schools whether you have children in school or not, find about their record of exclusionary discipline and any disparities in its application. Organize and inform your community members about issues in your schools. Insist in school board meetings that your schools change to a positive behavior support school. Volunteer for programs like the after-school leadership club. Books on peer mediation are available online. Volunteer as a mentor or classroom helper in your local school, early learning center or local com-munity center. Adopt ideas from here and make them your own. These ideas can be adapted to use with your own children and grandchildren. Also, contact your city and county courts to propose more diversion or dismissal opportunities for youth. Adult offenders in Arizona have more access to more lenient and creative sentencing than juveniles. Contact your state legislators and insist that they revamp the current punitive juvenile justice policies making them habilitative and rehabilitative in nature with natural supports as opposed to incarceration. Including parent support and education is essential. Please, consider helping dismantle the school-to-prison pipeline because *all* children are *our* children.

In this current culture of heightened racial and political tensions, children and adults can be taught/learn to share the love, and just like the cousins described above, young people or even adults can be supportive of their cousins. A key component to change to master or adapt social-emotional mastery to new situations is to find out what is important to other people and yourself. Learn the hot buttons of people and help them or yourself to use those passions to make a difference or survive anywhere. People can work, go to school, or interact with anyone if they do not have to take them home. Children, tweens, teens, and adults can stand up and use the affirmations /responses above modified to fit their situation. I don't participate in gossip and walking away works in the workplace as well as it does in school. Come on, cousin, friend, co-worker, have lunch with us when you notice someone being bullied or alienated. Everyone can come together and play their way to success and help dismantle the school-to-prison pipeline, thus creating a more positive future for *all*!

Bio

Diana Culver, M.Ed., Ph.D., is a single mother of 10 diverse children for over 40 years. She is a mother first, entrepreneur, advocate for her children and others. This chapter is loosely based on her dissertation. She is a self-proclaimed civil rights superhero (50-year activist) with a cape and love glasses. She is an educator of children, families and the community. Her current remaining business is KIDS KLUB, Inc., quality early learning combined with after-school program and infant and toddler programs. Her previous businesses were primarily owning and operating small budget apartment complexes. Her learning opportunities were a restaurant where she lost her shirt and a senior matchmaking service before computers, not so great! She is the author of Real Families, Voice, Value and Respect, empowering parents and professionals to advocate for their children and those they serve. She is also a co-author of the Amazon bestseller *Love Meets Life*. She has prior experience in corrections, sales, management and with intellectually challenged people. Diana is a people builder, and her passion is helping children have the best childhood possible and best prospects for the future. Contact: dculverphd@gmail.com, 520-560-5016

A Walk in the Seasons of Time
By Geneva Dantes

I walk through the woods, the seasons of time and marvel at the likeness. It is the path we walk. It is the journey made of our choices, our hope to grow love in our universe, in our world, in our life. It is the walk that keeps us moving forward.

Know this is the path of possibilities. This is the path to create your beauty. The path now even and straight, easy to see. Your heart is light, and hope is full. With brave intent, bow to the grace of your being. Be true.

To what sings newness in your life, what is clear? The start of the season, the start of the walk begins with clarity. The time to choose what the coming seasons unfold. This foundation establishes your roots. What is strong, what is supported, what no longer sings the sweet song that pleases your soul? Of those around you, how do they feel? Do they bring you light, challenge your grit, or emit a sad flow? What does each offer to your life, your soul, your being? Is this part of the new to carry on, or is it time to be something, someone anew? Now is the season to choose.

Spring

I walk through the woods in the Springtime, the season of time, all possibilities. The child-like remembrance of new and exciting. A deep breath in, the air fresh and clean. The ground is soft. Take choice in planting. The finest your heart imagines. A moment breathes in your desire. This moment important, as all the moments to come. Intention set now will be your path. A path on destiny's many paths to come. Kindly consider the one you set today. You are important, your happiness key. Look to the future but stay near. Other paths are choices for other days.

Who is the person, the being within? That which lives silent, wish to belong; what to survive, what o leave hare? To plant now and let grow, to be which your soul desires. A soul in a world of souls who long to sing. What part to provide, what part will you bring? To grow, to be greater than one in this place, where many grow strong. Look around, the trees to see, there are many with unity sing. Swaying together, weather each storm, a home for beauty, a safe place to own.

Plant now the dream of dreams. With faith to grow and strength surrounds. Your path, your garden in two, one is the same. Your thoughts clear, your passion strong, your desire for good stands. To be the seeds, to reach with roots, all is here with faith abide. Behold the sunrise with dreams.

Summer

I walk through the woods in the Summertime, the season of time to tend and grow. Yes, here among the tall trees standing. Deep roots support the reach to nurture grace. The ground with layers of ages cover, enrich what would blossom here. Full of hope for seeds are sown. You planted wisely beneath and shelter. Birds sing and bring life on wings as others come to guard what grows, to give part to your heart's desire. Those know what is true, what serves you best. What supports you and the world that tests will strengthen.

To plant is merely a start. That which chokes to be gone, that which withers needs to be strong. More decisions to make as this life you grow. The water of life, love, more than hope with grace you bestow. Pause again to consider happiness. Will this grow wild or keep contained? Have seeds wandered, have they survived, a season of change to make your soul thrive? Choices are still yours to make, to keep your garden that which remains.

Know your future that you thrive. This path has seen the spring of hope and seeds sown in the soil chosen, on the path grown. Take comfort in knowing your destiny is alive. This but a path, whether great or small; take care to walk it with love by your side. Many in the woods are here to help, to see them to know them, but a whisper to call them near. They love you, for you they fly, they run, they wait to remain by your side. Call for love and faith, as no one alone will face the journey, the path to walk.

Behold your path, your garden grown. Though patched with mist and turns unseen. This is yours; it is how you have grown. The sun bright from above to shine on you, your path to light. The light of seeing and nurture growth, to all it shines to all on earth. From heaven, it journeys far for light to cause winds to blow, a concert with earth clouds form. A cycle of life within life is formed. Behold, the sunrise with growth.

Fall

I walk through the woods in the Fall time, the season of time to sow and celebrate. Standing here, a time to harvest a time to sing. Your dreams, your seeds, your nurturing. Your toils, your struggles. Your laughter, your tears. Your creation now ready to embrace. Celebrate that which grew. Celebrate your life. The path, the season to dance, happiness inhale.

Joy of the bounty, for you all are bountiful. Your seeds have grown to what you had them become. Embrace, gather in your arms, for this is yours. As you walk this path of gathering, accept all that greets. Look close to find the unexpected love provides. You may wonder why this is a blessing to be. What grace, what magic now I see.

Some have withered, though extra care, some have bloomed beyond despair. What seeds were planted all mine I now see. Anguish not for those without bloom. In a time of blossom, what has matured, ready for life, ready and right. Of the bounty none left behind, your growth gathers all to shine, to reveal and sing with glee. These you have grown from your seeds of choice. Nurtured with all you gave and called for those on sorrow days, to keep this strong for what it is meant to be.

Walk this path with open eyes, behold your truth. To this season all comes, your soul opens wide. The good, the sad, to joy brought by thought, has growth on this path, in this spot. Save all you have to contemplate. Now is the time to finish this place of growth, this path of choice. Leave none behind. It is all important to you, part of you, and that you know.

Tall trees with colors to please, cradle your creation. These arms with you embrace the whole. Those who help you welcome in what is here. They dance, they sing around the fire, and dawn brings the time to close. What is done is complete. Behold, the sun sets and rests in the peace of knowing the harvest completes.

Winter

I walk through the woods in the Wintertime, the season of time to reflect and know. On what you have, know true love has comfort here. For in your bosom, your life is full, your heart beats strong, your soul soars and endures. All gathered to you, you partake.

The time of wisdom to embrace with love, eyes open, ears, heart, and soul to unfold the truths of seasons past. What is done is part of you, more wisdom, more strength, more peace to shine. Your grace extends the togetherness of why you love so deeply. Alone your heart will sing and share the truth of what you know, what did grow and bloom. Although some to see it not, look close for what it brought to you, your life and somehow needs. What is beyond what we cannot see rings a distant sound.

Grow in wisdom and knowledge for what you have done, you walked, you soared, you gave love to everyone who walked with you though ones unseen. Gave help to you, gave help to them. Clearly told a whispered sigh, the quiet that fills the space now sown, now used, not stored for future comes. To all who wish, to all who dream, to all to walk the journey. Not all survive. It is time to rest. Time to reflect. What have you learned, how have you grown?

Not all is as you planned, but all is as it should. Look back at your seasons. This was your walk? Were your seeds true, was your toil enough? Revel in the wisdom you have gained. Know it as your best. Take not today to change the choices made on that path on that day. No tear for more, no wish for less. The tree bends, the tree is straight, trees in solo stand. Others close as one communion strong. Embraced by sun and moon and rain to all reaches. Each played its part, the path, the season, the time.

I walk through the woods the seasons of time and marvel at the likeness. Be kind to your life, your self and know your seeds your choices were of that time. You did what you could with what you had. Your choices were based on that day. To walk the walk, the path of life. To sow the seeds, to grow what comes, to gather, to know. The sun sets on the path of time. Take joy in knowing; behold the sunrise, the sun does shine.

Bio

Born in rural America, I recall words of wisdom. First from my high school English teacher who told us with certainly, 'Everyone has a story to tell.' Later in life, the words of Dr. Wayne Dyer, 'Do not die with your music in you.' Such words inspire me to write, whether a newsletter article or a technical paper. Yes, technical. I also write to give my right side a sporting chance to speak. With Gemini as a sun sign and Pisces as a rising sign, surely my communication is intended to inspire.

Still One
By Kayleon Dortch-Elliott

Ifthere is one thing we will always need, it is community.

We were not created to navigate life alone; neither should we. Many of us have experienced the beauty of community just as often as we have the beast in it. Our disappointment when the reality of our relationships doesn't reflect our expectations speaks to the innate longing for the community we all possess. We have discovered a never-ending paradox of peace and tension, loyalty and betrayal, appreciation and regret. *Why can't we all just get along?* As complex as human relationships are, it is our responsibility to identify barriers that stand in our way and take the necessary steps to break them down.

Identifying Barriers

There are three major barriers that hinder us from embracing genuine community. The first barrier is vulnerability, a word just as difficult to pronounce as to practice. If only we could engage in a community without having to be vulnerable, we might feel safer. This safety does not refer to boundaries set to protect us from life-threatening situations, but to the safety we feel when we are known by others only to the extent of which we are most comfortable. The possibility of being vulnerable in a community is frightening to many. Indeed, so frightening that we become more inclined toward superficial connect-ions that come and go with the wind than deep-seated ones that do nothing for our ego but everything for our hearts and souls. Fear of vulnerability paints a picture of everyone whom you have yet to meet as a threat. However, the irony is you may feel that many who *already* know you don't truly know who you are. So ultimately, neither option has the safety you seek, considering that there is no guarantee that you will be known as you desire to be known.

With that in mind, take a minute to reflect on how you have changed and grown over the years. Is it reasonable to expect those who met you in adulthood to know and understand you in light of your childhood trauma? Do all your childhood friends fully connect with where you are now as an adult? Unfortunately, the answer to both questions is no. Because we have worked to become aware of who we are and how we have evolved over the years, we automatically assume that everyone who has met us (whether in childhood or adulthood) has the capacity to understand and know us fully. However, this is practically impossible, as even someone who has known you your entire life is not aware of your internal emotions and thoughts. Furthermore, since we have unconscious thoughts that we ourselves are not aware of, how can we expect those around us to truly know us? Rather than resenting them or automatically attributing separation to outgrowth, it is helpful to recognize and acknowledge that the disconnect is unlikely something they would have chosen if they could. Furthermore, let the reality that we all have experienced the fear of vulnerability be a source of empathy as opposed to an excuse. Consider it as you open yourself up to new relationships and possibly even seek to go beyond the surface in existing relationships. You are not the only one being known; so is the other person.

The second barrier is the societal glorification of isolation in the name of independence. We are influenced by a culture that promotes self-sufficiency, with individuals climbing up success ladders alone first and then turning around to help others. While there are occasions where we may have to walk alone, it is the motive behind isolation that matters most. Are we walking alone because we have to, or are we distrustful and afraid of the accountability found in community? Many times, we strive for independence because we know that in a community, it is not all about us. Other times we're afraid of being controlled or manipulated, but we've failed to embrace the option of inter-dependence. With inter-dependence comes the freedom to lean on others and be leaned on without control getting in the way.

The third barrier is *othering*, a process whereby specific individuals or groups are labeled insignificant or inferior; they are demeaned, belittled, and treated peripherally. *Nothing special to see here!* Ordinary, to say the least. Somehow we have gone from canceling memberships and subscriptions to canceling people. Anyone that doesn't fit the aesthetically pleasing life we desire for the world to see is deemed unworthy of our time or energy. We have appointed social media as a judge over our relationships, and when not used for positivity, it does nothing but boldfaces marginalization and highlights vilification in yellow. We have equated loyalty, trust, and worth to likes, statuses, and friend requests. It is not uncommon for individuals to have a seemingly genuine connection offline but only be friends on social media for the optics. And if we're honest, sometimes mutual friends are merely people who deem the same person as a mutual enemy. It is fair to conclude that othering is dominant in our culture and that much of the judgments made are based on a one-sided scale. What would happen, though, if we started holding ourselves to the same standards we hold others to? Perhaps grace wouldn't be as difficult a concept to grasp, more or less practice.

Eliminating Barriers

Now that we've identified three major barriers, what steps should we take to overcome them? The most important yet underused tool to embracing community is the art of holding space. Holding space involves making room for someone to express themselves without judgment, control of the narrative, or expectation of anything in return. It is characterized by active listening, presence (emotional, physical, mental), respect, humility, and empathy. The person for which space is held has permission to be, speak, and feel. At the surface, holding space for ourselves and others does not seem productive or effective in the moment. It would be considered ordinary, possessing no special features beyond what is normal, commonplace, or standard. Regular. Simple. Plain. Mediocre. This consideration may very well be the reason it is not commonly practiced.

When was the last time someone held space for you?

When was the last time you held space for someone else?

When was the last time you held space for yourself?

If you are having a hard time answering or cannot remember, it might be time to start. It is necessary to embrace the beauty in holding space if you desire to see a notable difference in the quality of our relationships. Contrary to popular belief, there are life-changing effects found in ordinary disciplines.

Holding space for yourself:

Go in a room by yourself and meditate, journal, or pray. Don't worry about whether what you are saying or writing makes sense. Don't focus on how it looks or sounds or why you shouldn't be feeling the way you feel. You are, and denying it will only have you back in the same position in little to no time. Pay attention to your surroundings. Your senses. Your breathing and heartbeat. Where you are in life. Call to mind what's hurting you, and then reflect on what's helping you. What have you overcome? What lessons have you learned? Who are you as a result of your experiences? What makes you proud of yourself? Who are you aside from the noise? When the dust settles, what's left in your life? What matters to you? *Who* matters? During this time, you are not trying to alter your reality but rather acknowledging what is. You are not beating yourself up for anything, but replacing every condemning thought with the truth of who you are, and if you believe in God, who God is in your life as well as the freedom He has made possible. Prioritizing time to check in with and hold space for yourself is vital. You cannot effectively embrace community if you are not self-aware.

Holding space for others:

Be intentional in every interaction, even in those you consider to be ordinary or nothing special. When someone confides in you, listen. Don't try to read between the lines and hear what they're not saying. Take what they're saying at face value and be there for them. Don't label their feelings as right or wrong, and don't think about advice to offer them. You may not have experienced their exact situation, but you have been in the position of needing someone, and you remember what you needed. Be that for them. Be who you wish you had in your situation. Someone who isn't coming with preconceived notions or answers. Someone who is simply holding space because we all need and deserve it. The reality is we only have enough love for others as we have for ourselves, and too often, we approach situations, conversations, and community at large solely based on what's in it for us. The art of holding space is viewing and treating humans as people beyond what they can offer.

Holding space makes it possible for authentic, long-lasting community. Mastering this art requires humility, empathy, honesty, intentionality, contentment, an appreciation of simplicity, and most importantly, grace. We face immense pressure daily, striving to be accepted by our behaviors, style of dress, neighborhoods, degrees, titles, credit scores, and more. But grace wouldn't be grace if it had to be earned, and that's what makes it unique—it's completely counter-cultural. In our workplaces, families, churches, homes, and societies, there are expectations of having it all together all the time.

But what about days when it's difficult to show up?

When it takes more than an alarm to get you out of bed?

When you feel alone in a crowded room?

When imposter syndrome gets the best of you?

When you feel like the worst vers---

Let's stop here. It's interesting to see how often we compartmentalize ourselves, identifying versions of ourselves based on others' standards as well as our own standards of how we would like to be portrayed. The reality is there are no best or worst versions of yourself, and even if there were, it'd be impossible for you to show up as one without the other close behind. There is just you. And that is where the practicality of grace, holding space, and community begins: acknowledging the fullness of who you are because you realize you need grace just as much on your bad days as you do good ones.

Grace is finding contentment and beauty in the ordinary. It is loving those who have nothing extraordinary to give us. It is involved in our every day, always hidden in plain sight. Grace is not meant to be accidental or a mere first aid kit we finally run to once we've tried all our other options. It is not to be tossed in the backseat or trunk of our lives just in case. Whether we realize it or not, there is never a time we don't need grace. As a matter of fact, it is when we feel most self-sufficient and capable that we need it the most. We can offer grace to ourselves and experience the grace of God, but there is something special about receiving grace from another person. You may view the offering of grace to yourself as a practice of denial or the offering of grace from God as an expression of pity, but when another human being extends grace, the fact that it is a gift cannot be denied.

Regarding the basis of God's compassion, David wrote in Psalm 103:14, "For he knows our frame; he remembers that we are only dust." When we hold space and extend grace, we make it known that we remember our frame, too. Embracing community becomes less difficult when you remember that everyone around you is no different than you. We may not resemble one another according to the external standards by which we choose relationships, but in our nature, we are one. Ordinary, but still one.

Bio

Kayleon Dortch-Elliott is a lifelong lover of the arts and first began writing in her early years of life. Consultant, designer, speaker, and author of *One Day at a Time: Remaining in Step,* Kayleon resides in North Carolina with her husband and daughter. She has earned a Bachelor of Arts degree in Christian Ministry and is a Master of Theological Studies Candidate at Regent University. Her educational background in theological research and writing has given her a unique perspective and base from which to approach diverse topics. Kayleon is the founder of By Grace Not Perfection LLC where she assists entrepreneurs with personal, brand, and professional development through a variety of services. She is also the host of My Sentiments Exactly, a podcast and community dedicated to addressing stigma, raising awareness, and facilitating the necessary but difficult conversations that stand in the way of genuine community. Off the clock, Kayleon enjoys spending time with her family, traveling, reading, solving logic puzzles, and indulging in chocolate-covered pretzels.

Ways to Stay Connected:
Website: www.bygracenp.com
Email: bygracenp@gmail.com
Social Media: @bgnpllc

Everyday Unconditional Love
By Rina Escalante

As a child, the insides of doctors' offices and hospitals were commonplace because of my immune system, which is to say, my overactive immune system that thought everything was attacking my body. When I say everything, I mean food, dust, mold, feathers, animals and the wet climate (fog) were not good for me. Basically, the environment I lived in, my beautiful home, my city. I was born in a special and scenic place. Even Tony Bennett thought so because he left his heart in San Francisco. As lovely, mysterious and romantic as San Francisco is in my memory, the cold and wet climate was not particularly conducive for a child that suffered from asthma. My parents made the decision and moved us further down the peninsula, where the weather was better. Thankfully, this is possible in the Bay Area because of micro-climates. My dad was promoted through the United Airlines Maintenance Base, so he still needed to be within a commuting distance, and our grandparents still lived in San Francisco.

Back in 1978, we moved to a young, planned community about fifteen minutes South of the Maintenance Base and about thirty minutes South of San Francisco named Foster City. What an absolute blessing! When the house hunting began, we would hear how our mom wanted a big white house with columns on the front. Our Foster City house met her dream, was lovely and spacious. It had a front lawn and bordered on one side by five large pine trees. Our backyard was just as nice. It also had large, beautiful pine trees, room to run around and eventually, my mom built out the landscaping, so it was calming and peaceful.

I was attached to my City and the beautiful architecture of the old homes. My mom would say that when I was little (pre-kinder), I would always talk about "mi casita de Army" (my little house on Army *street*), which is now Cesar Chavez Boulevard. Our houses always had such personality. My parents had a good eye and always found beautiful homes. I loved (and still do) all the details of the old San Francisco houses, the beveled edged windows and built-in mirrors, the dimensions in the ceilings, baseboards and doors, all the ornate doorknobs, the built-in dining room cabinet that also had all the beveled windows and pretty knobs, there was so much to look at and appreciate. Foster City was a new planned community, and many of the houses around town were the same. They did not have the detail of the San Francisco houses. I used to call them Lego houses. When they would build up a new neighborhood, a caravan of huge semi-trucks would drive into town with prebuilt sides and sections of houses framed out. The construction teams just had to put them together, piece by piece.

We moved to Foster City when I was in my first semester of eighth grade, my final year at St. Peter's. I had felt so attached to my classmates and my little school. We had been attending school together since first grade, and our beautifully diverse school made me feel content and relaxed. I fit in with everyone as most of us were children of immigrants and bilingual. I had been one of the first girls to serve as an altar girl, I had been an active member of student government and had been involved in tutoring the lower grades. St. Peter's was my community.

During the first few weeks of moving down the peninsula, my dad did the best he could to help me cope. He used to get up at the crack of dawn to drive me up to San Francisco to my grandparents' house. My grandfather, Vito Chepe, would make me breakfast and walk me to school. After school, there was Vito waiting for me, and we would walk back to their house together. I would get rewarded by my grandmother Vita Clemen's cooking. I would do my homework and wait for my dad. He would visit for a bit, and then we would head home. I do not think I lasted with that routine for much of an extended period. I was getting exhausted. I made the decision to go to public school in Foster City just like my other three siblings. I was so heartbroken, leaving what had been so familiar to me for most of my life at that point. I appreciated my dad for making the sacrifice for me with all my young being. He let me make my own decision of what was the best thing for me, and I knew he supported me no matter what choice I made.

When I enrolled at my new school, Bowditch Middle School, there were two people I knew, my brother and our neighbor Kathy who were both two grades lower than me. The three of us rode our bikes to school together. Kathy did her best to include me with her group of friends to help me get acclimated. She made sure we would have a meeting place for lunch, so I would not wander around alone. I still have a vivid memory of one of her homemade lunches that she kindly shared with me, fried chicken! My mouth still waters thinking about her mom Linda's fried chicken goodness. She giggled and said, "I'm going to have to invite you over and have some of that chicken freshly made. If you like it cold, wait till you try my mom's chicken right after she makes it." Good thing Kathy lived right next door! Maybe living in Foster City was not going to be so bad after all.

Acts of kindness, caring, and unmotivated love leave impacts on people's lives.

After I was at my new school for a few weeks, I, along with a handful of other new students, needed to take a group picture for the yearbook. Coming from a Catholic elementary school, I had no idea what a yearbook was. I just went where they directed me. Memory serves me that after that experience, I began to make more friends in my grade, kids that are now parents and grandparents too. The blessing for me has been to become an adult and to still be in touch with many of the friends I met during that transition in my life. I completely attribute their friendships to my ability to adapt to my new home in Foster City. A handful of these special friendships are what sustains me today. Without these open, kind and loving spirits in my life, I do not know how I would have made it this far. I credit my ability to survive life's trials to these special women.

One of those loving, long-term friendships is with Tamara. She was the first person I had ever met, at least that I knew of at that point, who had been adopted. She has *adopted* me into her life and her family. My daughters and grand-children call her "Auntie."

There have been many times during our friendship, where her selfless acts of love have saved my life emotionally, literally and figuratively. Her home was my *healing space* when I was completely broken back in 2013, standing on the brink of complete breakdown and has since been my stable force and refuge whenever I need it. Tamara brought me back to life, taught me how to live my life with care and lovingness towards myself and my body by exposing and teaching me how to eat clean.

During this time of self-discovery, I began to learn about what was good for my body and what was not. Tamara was guiding me on all the different ways to eat clean or healthier. In other words, 'was I allergic or did I have intolerances to certain foods?' I ended up discovering that a lot of the foods in my diet were fighting against me. Just like with autoimmune disease, if you have one, you are more than likely to have more. I was already lactose intolerant, and I soon realized that I did have many more food intolerances. We went through a lot of testing and deducing foods that were alright to eat and what was not. I think the toughest for me was eliminating sourdough bread, the tragedy! What type of San Franciscan is allergic to their sourdough? I raise my hand, me! Once I cleaned out my diet, I was able to determine what I could and could not eat; I now eat a Paleo diet. I lost a lot of weight, and I no longer had allergies, thanks to eliminating wheat.

Tamara's home is always a welcome respite to all of us who need a helping hand in our lives, those who just need a place to stay overnight and to those, like me, who *need* it. I say her home is our *Haven*. Webster defines haven: 1) harbor, port 2) a place of safety: refuge. A refuge is defined as 1) a shelter or protection from danger or distress 2) a place that provides shelter or protection. Silly of me to think I was the only one she "adopted."

What I have witnessed is that Tamara helps in any and all ways she can. She shares herself and knowledge and gives guidance (she calls it "gentle nudging") to her friends and family with her special *unconditional love*. I think everyone needs a Tamara!

The *beauty, purity and selflessness* of *unconditional love* is that you do things because they come naturally to you, it is part of who you are, and you do not think or expect anything in return. You perform these acts because doing so is innate. It is part of your soul and being. Not to do so would be against your aligned purpose. This type of deep discourse may make you sense that your life and however you look at your journey, would *feel* off balance. You may begin to act against yourself, and it can manifest itself in too many ways to count.

I say anyone has the ability to give with unconditional love; it takes special people to give us examples of how to do so right in front of us. We just need to open our eyes, ears and heart. If we listen and feel with our hearts openly, their vibration will reverberate from every action they take, which makes it easier to receive their positive, giving and kind energy. I am sure each of us can tune in or knows one of these special souls.

That person or people can be loving grandparents who assist their son and granddaughter, it can be a caring dad who wants to help his child cope during a family transition, it can be a young neighbor who does things out of her heart space because that is who she is, or it can be your best friend who loves you unconditionally, just because you are you.

Positivity and kindness are important attributes, and they can identify someone's choice on how they live their lives. When you begin with kind and loving acts for yourself, those vibrations will emanate from your entire soul, you will glow as you are walking in communion with love. Loving yourself will glow from your every pore, and that love will be easily shared as it will become how you live and walk your journey. You become that pebble that gets tossed in a pond. Not only will you give off a similar type of vibration, but your acts will inspire more acts of kindness on their way towards unconditional love, and just think, *you* become that trajectory. How glorious would our journey be if we had more special souls to walk with?

Do not be afraid to be that changemaker in the social, familial and friendship circles you travel in. I doubt if kindness, caring, compassion and unconditional love will ever go out of style. *Be the change!*

Bio

Rina Escalante is the daughter of immigrants from El Salvador. Her family immigrated to the Mission District in San Francisco in the late 1950s and early 1960s. She believes that if you surround yourself with positive energy, you have the power to make anything possible. She shares her life experiences in her storytelling with the intention the reader will know they are not alone on their life journey. Rina is in the process of attaining her certifications in Reiki energy healing and studying Shamanic healing with native plants so she can open a healing center in So. Lake Tahoe. You can contact Rina at rinaesca@gmail.com.

The Ties That Bind
By Karen Gabler

"Mommy, I want a big brother."

My mother stroked my hair as she tucked me into bed. She masked her amusement at the impossibility of my request as she distracted me with a hug. "We'll see, honey."

At the age of five, I had been without my father for more than three years. A stomach ache that wouldn't go away led to a diagnosis of terminal cancer. My 30-year-old father left my life as quickly as I had entered his.

Like many who pass "before their time," my young father's legacy shone bright. Family members shared stories of a man who could do no wrong. Charismatic and funny; bright and ambitious. An engineer's mind with an artist's hands. A deep love for his mother, for whom he would do anything. A magnet for female attention, enhanced by a Southern boy's charm. A Marine pilot's confidence and swagger, tempered by an unwavering concern for the well-being of others.

He built airplane models as a child and grew up to tinker with plane engines. Blessed with natural athleticism, he had a good-natured competitive streak. He played football with zeal; my grandmother spent hours pasting newspaper clippings into a hefty album of his achievements.

He fell deeply in love with the daughter of a decorated Marine officer. Married in dress blues and white silk, they exited the chapel to begin their new life together beneath the Arch of Swords held high by my father's military brothers. Like many young couples in the 1960's, they quickly turned their attention to starting a family.

As the first grandchild and the first girl in my father's family of boys, I was born to great fanfare. My father nicknamed me "Miss America" and insisted that I would become the President someday. Faded photos reveal that my feet rarely touched the ground; everyone wanted a chance to hold the baby.

The sudden death of my young father shattered his family as well as the community. The loss of this golden boy was devastating in itself, but leaving behind his 24-year-old wife only two weeks prior to his daughter's second birthday was unfathomably tragic. My mother took me to seek refuge at her parents' home in Chicago. My father's family expressed understanding, but privately lamented her decision to take me away from "home" and turn me into a "Yankee."

Growing up hundreds of miles from my Southern roots, the shadow of my father's death followed me. My mother remarried and I was adopted by her second husband. Questions about my parents confounded me: my explanation of having "two dads" typically resulted in sadness or confusion for the listener, neither of which I was equipped to handle. Visits to my Southern relatives were a reminder of the family's collective grief, frozen in time. My great-aunt held my face and said "you have your father's nose," as she cried. I sat in my grandmother's rocking chair; she recalled that she once rocked my father in the same chair. We watched home videos of holiday celebrations I had missed throughout the years. I watched with resentment, feeling cheated by the lost life they represented.

I began to move through the world somewhat detached from reality, uncertain how to live in the life I had been given. It was as if my life splintered in two when my father left this world. In one existence, I was a Southern belle, the only daughter of a man known and loved by everyone in the community and growing up with the confidence of a girl who can do no wrong in her daddy's eyes. In another, I was a suburban Northerner who grew up as the adopted daughter of an immigrant's son, sharing my home with two sisters (and without the big brother I had begged my mother to provide). In one life, my loving mother would have been doted on by a charming and playful husband. In the life handed to us, she struggled with loss, divorce and cancer, known for her selfless love for others but always touched by a tinge of unspoken sadness.

I began to lose touch with my father's distant family over time. We were connected by a thread of grief and loss, bound only by our collective love for the young man who touched our lives so deeply before leaping out of this world. I moved to Hawaii with my mother and sister, finished law school and began practicing in a Honolulu law firm.

When my mother finally succumbed to the cancer cells invading her body, I grieved not only the loss of my best friend, but also the secondary loss of my father. My mother took with her the stories of their courtship and marriage, and their delight at my birth. She left behind boxes of love notes and grainy photos to remind me of a giddy young couple in love, who were almost children themselves when they decided to become parents.

Over the years, I consoled myself by making lists of reasons that my life was blessed because of, not merely in spite of, the early loss of my parents. If I had not lost my father, I would have been deprived of the sisters I found through my mother's second marriage. If I had not lost my mother in Hawaii, I never would have moved to California and met the man of my dreams, who brought a son to me and then held my hand as I gave birth to our own little princess.

As I embraced the joys in my life, I pulled away from my fantasies of the life I should have, could have, lived under different circumstances. And yet, I felt unmoored in the world. I was orphaned, left behind by the people who brought me into being. Without someone in my life to tell me who I was and where I came from, I didn't know who to be or where to go.

On September 7, 2017, I was home with bronchitis, scrolling through emails from my law office to see if anything urgent required my attention. I opened a message from a man named Matthew, who introduced himself as an attorney in Florida. Suspecting an impending legal dispute, I quickly scanned the email.

" . . . . My DNA testing and other research has led me to believe there is a high probability that your father is also my father."

I read the email again . . . and again.

I had a brother. A *big* brother.

Later discussions filled in some of the blanks. My father was in a relationship with a woman four years before he met my mother; they drifted apart when he headed to flight training school. Matt's unwed mother, a product of 1960's propriety and judgment, lived with a friend out of town to hide her unexpected pregnancy and agreed to give up her baby to adoption with a loving couple.

Matt and his family flew to California to meet me in person. I watched the window with eager anticipation, wondering what it would be like to meet a brother I had never known. I felt as if my father was standing nearby, waiting to see his children meet for the first time.

When the doorbell rang, I opened the door and looked into Matt's eyes. In a moment that felt like an eternity, I scanned his face and thought, "wow…he really does have my nose!" My heart was pounding as we held each other in a long hug. I wished that I could download his life story into my memory banks to give my mind a chance to catch up with my heart.

We spent several hours going through boxes of photos, military memorabilia and mementos from our father's life. Matt filled in researched details of our father's military career; I shared the stories I'd been told. As we looked at photos of our father holding me, I was suddenly struck by what we had lost. My father never had a chance to hold his son, Matt was never able to know his father, I grew up without my brother. I wondered what life would have been like if we had been given time to spend it with each other.

When my brother found me, I questioned whether this new relationship could fill the hole that my father's death left in my life. I wondered whether I expected Matt to bring my father back to me and reminded myself that Matt didn't have the chance to grow up with him any more than I did. Matt could not tell me his stories, nor could he let me into my father's heart. Instead, Matt and I were joined in our unfulfilled desire for answers and connected by our mutual loss of the man who helped bring us to life.

To my surprise, however, Matt did bring my father back to me. By launching his journey into our father's history, Matt filled in gaps in my own information. He spoke to extended family members and reminded me of their stories. He gave me a reason to dust off photos and boxes I had shoved away in closets, like the feelings I shoved into the recesses of my heart. He allowed me to rediscover our father: the things that intrigued him, the way others saw him, how he showed up in the world.

Through his willingness to share himself with me, Matt also allowed me to see all the ways in which he is very much his father's son. Like our father, Matt served in the Marine Corps and later became a pilot. Channeling our father's compulsion to tinker with machinery and engines, Matt also built model airplanes as a child, later building his own airplane from the ground up. His love of flying shines in his eyes when he talks about it; I can imagine how our father must have sounded when he talked about his flights as well.

Matt inherited our father's quick wit and intelligence. Like our father, Matt is tenacious and driven; he pored over hours of research to build an accurate story of our family as he searched for his own past. Matt and I each became lawyers, and we share a love of history, as did our father. Over time, I have come to know my brother as a man of integrity and courage. He is witty, intelligent and charming. He is caring, and he loves his family deeply. He honors his wife and children and celebrates their life together.

As Matt and I shared information and stories with each other, I realized that I didn't need Matt to help me find my father. Instead, I needed him to help me find *myself*. In finding his own history, Matt brought mine back to me as well. By sharing his process of learning about where he came from and who he is, Matt allowed me to reconnect with where I came from and who I am.

Matt and I share a similar path; we each grew up detached from where we were "supposed to be" when we were born. And yet, the similarities between us and the traits we share with our father have taught me that we are exactly who we were meant to be. Our place in the world is anchored by who we are, not the people or places around us. Our lives may take many divergent paths, but the ties that bind are stronger than the winds that blow.

I no longer feel unmoored in this world, and no longer feel abandoned. I know who I was and who I am. Like my father and brother, I have integrity and courage. I am witty, intelligent and charming. I am caring, and love my family deeply. I honor my husband and children, and celebrate our life together. I have parents, grandparents, sisters, aunts, uncles, cousins, nieces and nephews.

And I have a brother.

A *big* brother.

Bio

Karen Gabler is an attorney, intuitive mentor and psychic medium. She is also a best-selling author, teacher and inspirational speaker. Karen is passionate about encouraging others to find their highest purpose and live their best lives. She mentors her clients through a variety of personal and business questions, marrying her practical legal and business experience with her intuitive ability to receive information and guidance from higher sources. She also facilitates connections with clients' loved ones in spirit. Karen conducts workshops, spiritual services and presentations on a variety of business, spiritual and personal development topics. Karen earned her Bachelor of Science in psychology from the University of Hawaii and her Juris Doctorate from the William S. Richardson School of Law at the University of Hawaii. She has pursued wide-ranging education in interpersonal development and the spiritual sciences, working with tutors from the prestigious Arthur Findlay College for the Psychic Sciences in England as well as with intuitives and psychic mediums throughout the United States. She is a WCIT in the Martha Beck Wayfinder life coaching program. She enjoys reading, hiking, horseback riding and spending time with her husband and two children. You can find Karen at www.karengabler.com.

In the Eye of the Hurricane
By Sarah Gabler

In March of 2020, I was nearing the end of my eighth-grade year in middle school. My thoughts were quickly turning to my upcoming high school experience. I was so excited to start my new life! When I entered high school, I was going to be a whole new version of myself.

Like many other young teenagers, middle school was not easy for me. I had experienced the pain caused by bullies, I "broke up" with a best friend who turned out to be manipulative and self-absorbed, and handled the pressures of a 10-hour day between classes and extracurricular activities, all while juggling a heavy load of homework and keeping up with my grades. Although I maintained an "A" average, it felt like a constant struggle.

Ready to put it all behind me, I was thrilled to be headed to high school. I had a new perspective on life from all my experiences in middle school. In my larger high school environment, almost no one would know who I was. I knew this was my chance to change the way I showed up in the world and the way others viewed me.

The week before spring break, we were informed that a new virus called "COVID-19" was spreading quickly. We moved to online schooling temporarily, and our teachers told us they would see us in a few weeks, expecting the crisis would pass by the time spring break was over.

For most of my schooling, I relied on my parents for support. They were the only ones who knew just what to do to calm me down when I was stressed, and they helped me when I didn't understand my school work. Along with my parents, I relied on my best friend, Lura. She was pulling out of another toxic friendship just as I was, and we became closer as we put our own happiness above the usual middle school drama. Lura and I did our homework together each day during our student support period, and we were so excited to appear together in our upcoming eighth grade musical. We looked forward to experiencing our promotion and beginning high school in the fall.

Unfortunately, we did not return to school after spring break. The school announced that our spring musical, promotion, and all other eighth grade events were being "re-worked" to fit the COVID-19 protocols. After a few weeks of chaos, while trying to finish school, Lura and I lost hope as we watched our plans dwindle. We knew that we weren't going to have graduation ceremonies or celebrations or appear on stage to showcase the results of our theater rehearsals. As I watched my graduation take place in a Zoom meeting from my couch, my life began to feel out of control.

I consoled myself with the thought of heading to high school in the fall when we could "get back to normal." Little did I know at that time that the disarray of my last semester of middle school would turn into a year-long shutdown. After a long summer spent staying home, I started high school online. Unfortunately, it didn't get much easier. In fact, it got a lot harder.

High school classes were segmented into morning and afternoon cohorts. Lura and I were in different cohorts; all my classes were in the afternoon, and hers were in the morning. This made it much harder for us to interact and support each other during the school day, leaving each of us feeling more alone. My schedule was not very forgiving. My first class lasted almost two and half hours, from 11:35 am to 2:00 pm. Another class quickly followed from 3:10 pm to 4:50 pm. This meant that lunch was delayed until late afternoon, leaving me with only an hour to eat and prepare for the next class.

Classes were held online through Zoom, and many students turned off their computer cameras, leaving me to stare at a series of black boxes on my laptop screen. I didn't know anyone in my classes and wasn't able to change that because I couldn't fully interact with other students. I had to figure out how to learn new subjects, how my new teachers liked to teach, and how to please them with my work, all while being miles away from them. I could no longer visit a classroom to ask a question, instead having to rely upon sending emails and waiting for a response.

Despite my struggles in learning to cope with this new way of life, I knew I still had my parents with me for support. I could talk to them for advice and get their help with my work. When I became stressed, they knew how to calm me down. When I realized that the COVID-19 pandemic would force my working parents to stay home as well, I was relieved because I knew it meant I would have my parents by my side. As long as I had my mom and dad with me, I would get through this.

As it turned out, the pandemic was not the family bonding experience I hoped it would be. I could always count on my dad to make me laugh and go on walks with me, but as an essential worker, my dad had to work with or without the pandemic. He was gone from 7:30 am until 5:30 pm each day. I told myself that at least I would have my mom with me. Things would be great when I was with my mom! We would have lunch together, she would help me with some of my work, and I could go to her when I needed to talk. Unfortunately, that didn't work out as planned, either. My mother's job required her to advise business clients on COVID-19 issues. With the pandemic exploding through the state, my mom was in her home office all day and had little time available to hang out with me. When I had a break, she was on the phone and couldn't talk to me. When she was able to pause for a minute, I was in class. When we could grab a quick lunch, it was 15 or 20 minutes of rushing through our food, asking each other how it was going before jumping back into our work.

Without my best friend or my parents by my side, I felt more alone than ever. I learned to cope with my "new normal" as much as possible for a while, but after a few months of doing physical education in front of a computer screen in my front hallway and algebra at my dining room table, I realized how much stress and depression I was shutting down inside of me. I am the kind of person who reacts to pressure by pushing myself through it, and I don't realize how much I am hurting until I am pushed over the edge.

Finally, I reached my breaking point, and everything changed for me. I had been living my "new normal" for a long time, and I just became fed up with it. I started to struggle mentally, to the point where I would cry almost every day because of the anger rising inside of me. I was angry at everything. I experienced all the emotions I worked through in middle school, but on a whole different level. When I became bored, I would eat to distract myself. It was easy to grab a quick snack when I didn't want to face my computer screen, but I felt like I was eating 10 pounds of sugar every day. This only made me more sluggish and angrier at myself for gaining weight.

I had no motivation to do anything. I didn't want to do my schoolwork, I didn't want to do my chores, I didn't want to exercise. Most of the time, I wouldn't leave the dining room table all day except to get food or go to the bathroom. I began behaving with a major attitude, and it started to affect my family as well. I knew I was living a very unhealthy lifestyle, and if I didn't change it, I would be putting myself at risk.

It took a long time for me to finally accept that I couldn't begin to feel better until I made a change in my choices and my attitude. I was tired of feeling worthless and like a waste of space all the time. I was tired of fantasizing about my ideal life and not doing anything to make it my reality. I needed to get in touch with my inner self and get my life back together.

I started by making a commitment to myself that I wasn't going to let my life fall into a slump just because the world around me was falling apart. I opened up to my mom and told her how I was feeling. I knew we were both experiencing the same struggles while cooped up in our house together, but I also knew that she was hiding it in an effort to support me. I asked her if we could spend more time talking to each other so we didn't bottle up our feelings.

I then looked at my school schedule and thought about how I could feel more organized and under control. I found an efficient way of keeping track of my work. I knew that most of the stress I was experiencing came from feeling overwhelmed about school and the difficulty of transitioning from in-person schooling to an online model. I realized that I had to stop being frustrated that I wasn't at school and start figuring out to adjust to my circumstances in a more productive way. I also realized that I needed to stop relying on other people to keep me on track and create stability for me. I needed to start relying on myself and motivating myself.

As I worked through each step, my mental health was improving, and I was feeling far less stressed about everything. I figured out how to keep track of my deadlines and stopped feeling overwhelmed all the time. I started making healthier choices about what I put into my body and felt my energy increase. I found a healthy balance between my school work and my personal activities, and I was managing it very well. I still encounter challenges, of course, but I know how to develop tools to get me through them, and I know that I can do anything.

Now that I have survived my first semester of "pandemic high school" and 2021 has officially begun, I recognize how far I have come since our first shutdown in March of 2020. I have realized that although 2020 was a horrible year for everyone across the world, it also taught me a lot about who I am and really helped me to grow as a person. Experiencing 2020 made me aware of my own strength and maturity. I have shown my teachers and parents that I can take on a lot of responsibility. More importantly, I have shown myself that I can do so, and I know I can rely upon myself to get through any difficulties that may come my way.

Thank you, 2020. You tried to knock me down, but you also taught me to get back up. I am now a stronger, healthier, calmer person. I will experience challenges in my life, but I know I will survive those challenges. I will no longer allow change to intimidate me, and I will embrace change with an open mind. Most of all, I now know myself, and I trust myself. In surviving the 2020 pandemic, I became my own best friend and my strongest supporter. In the eye of the hurricane, I learned to love myself.

Bio

Sarah Gabler is 14 years old and is in the ninth grade. She loves playing games with her family and traveling to new places. Sarah enjoys playing the ukulele and guitar, singing and dancing, and riding her horse. A lifelong artist, she is pursuing a scholastic pathway in graphic design and enjoys using creative outlets to express her artistic vision. She loves empowering people by helping them to recognize their true potential in the world and plans to do motivational speaking in the future. Sarah began exploring spiritual teachings and soul empowerment concepts when she was 10 years old and believes it has made her a better person today. It also has motivated her to find ways to live her best life and to help others on their journey to live their best lives as well. Sarah believes that even the smallest act of kindness can make someone's day, and she enjoys going out of her way to make others feel loved.

How Self-Care in Grief Taught Me Oneness
By Rosanne Groover Norris

Today, I saw Jesus. His baggy clothes were filthy. His gnarled hands clutched a pack of cigarettes. He shuffled along, mumbling to himself. I watched, from the car, as he approached my husband asking for money. My husband handed him a bill, and at that moment, I saw Jesus in him, too. He was clean and dressed in jeans. He drove a new truck and had plenty to eat. As I watched this exchange, it dawned on me that both men were the same. In their human form, although wildly different, both were somebody's child, father, brother, cousin, or friend. But on a deeper level, I recognized we are more than our human form. I understood how we are all connected on a soul level. We are all Jesus.

I started to look for Jesus in everyone and everything around me. I saw him walking down the street, working as a cashier, in the grocery store, in my puppy's loving eyes, and in nature. Jesus was simply everywhere, and I was one with him.

I didn't always feel this way. I was a good person, but I judged. I blamed. I could not see. But something happened to open my eyes to the oneness, the connection. To Jesus.

My son died.

I had a choice. I stood at a crossroad. One way was dark, leading to a life of pain, despair, and separateness. The other was a path of learning, growing, and knowing.

The path of Jesus.

I knew the second path would be the harder road to follow. It meant not giving up. It meant opening to the beauty, joy, and goodness of life. It meant, like Jesus, bearing the cross. I knew the path out of the darkness of grief would be difficult. I wasn't sure I could do it, but I decided to do the work for me, my son, my family, and the human collective. I knew self-care was the place to start.

Meditation was where I started my self-care. I had learned to quiet my mind in yoga. To me, the corpse pose, at the end of a session, was relaxing, but nothing more. After Lee passed, I couldn't function. I would sit and stare out the window for long periods of time. I watched the snowfall. I watched the birds at the feeder. I counted all the abandoned bird nests in the winter-bare trees. At first, I didn't realize I was meditating. I only knew that it felt good to be quiet and not think. In time, I started to go deeper, and in that stillness, healing started to germinate, in my heart, like a little seed. In time, I started to feel connected to humanity, nature, angels, guides, loved ones, the creator, and to Lee. And Jesus was at the center of this connection. Through meditation, I learned we are not separate but are all one, connected through our souls, which never die.

I have always been a reader, a lover of fiction, but now I am a seeker. Soon after Lee crossed, I started to read books about the afterlife. I was desperate to know what happened to him and where he went. I couldn't accept he could just vanish from the Earth without a trace. Through reading, I learned we continue, on the other side, with a full and rich life. I discovered once we cross, we don't lose connection with the people left behind. The reason we don't lose the connection is that we are all one. We are part of the source, linked by our souls. Our loved ones send all kinds of signs to prove this connection is real. I learned about soul families, soul groups, and how we choose roles that we want to play when we incarnate, for the valuable lessons we can learn from our human experience. Reading helped me to understand how we are connected. We are one, and everything we do, say, or even feel affects everyone. And once we realize that we are more alike than different, we will be willing to lend a helping hand to those in need rather than judging them. We can be like Jesus because we are Jesus.

Another self-care tool I used were mediums. I had many readings in the first two years after Lee transitioned. The mediums shared things they could not know about my son. This proved to me that life continued, on the other side. And this proof helped propel me further on the path toward healing. I learned that not only did Lee exist, but that I could still have a relationship with him. Knowing this furthered my realization that I am connected to everything and everyone on both sides of the veil, including my son. And because of that connection, I began to see the beauty in the people all around me. I started to see their souls. And I went to work on communicating with Lee, myself.

For me, journaling became the best way to work through my grief. I started to journal a few weeks after Lee crossed. I could safely express my pain on the page, and it didn't have to be coherent. I just wrote what I felt. Let it splat on the page. The more I wrote, the more my grief softened. And as the grief softened, the connection to Lee, everything, and everyone became stronger, and the realization that we are all one became clearer. I wrote twelve journals in the first two years after Lee crossed, which became a book. You don't have to write a book. You just have to purge the pain. Release the pressure. Seek the connection.

I found gentle yoga a great way to release the sadness that I held in my body. I didn't realize grief was so physical. The pain was excruciating. At times, I felt such a tightness in my chest, I could barely breathe. Yoga helped me to move the grief up and out of my body. It's also an opportunity to get quiet, and go within, and find the oneness with all that is. I often have stress-relieving tears during my practice, for which I am grateful.

I like this quote from the book *Wit & Wisdom From The Yoga Mat* by Rachel Scott.

"Practicing self-care is like washing the steps of your own temple."

I know grief will always be part of me, but self-care is the way to healing. And healing becomes knowing, and knowing becomes healing.

I recently saw Sara, a young, homeless woman who panhandles in the parking lot of the grocery store where I shop. My husband and I both give her money and/or food when we see her. Recently, as I put my groceries in my car, I saw Sara looking to the sky and wailing, "No one sees me. Everyone judges me. No one cares." I walked over and looked her in the eyes. "I see you. I care, and more importantly, God cares. At that moment, Jesus worked through me, letting Sara know that we are not alone. We are one. And for this, I am grateful.

In researching the definition of oneness, I came upon the quote from the Bible that always had perplexed me, but suddenly, I felt I understood the meaning. It is from John: 1:14.

"In the beginning was the Word, and the Word was with God, and the Word was God."

I understand that the Word is Jesus, and he came among us to bring us the Word and teach us the way to live. But, if we are all one, then aren't we, too, the Word?

I think John Lennon's line from The Beatles song, "I am The Walrus," sums up the idea of oneness perfectly.

"I am he as you are he as you are me, and we are all together."

Bio

Rosanne Groover Norris grew up in Binghamton, NY. She is the mother of five children, with one in spirit. She is also grandmother to six. She considers them all to be her best accomplishment in life. In January 2018, her middle, thirty-year-old son, Lee, succumbed to an accidental carbon monoxide poisoning in his home along with his dog, Buddy. This devastating event left her in a dark despair that she questioned was even survivable. Knowing she was at a crossroad, Rosanne embarked upon a quest to figure out her new reality. Through multiple modalities, she has learned that life is continuous, and we can still have a relationship with the people we love on the other side. This new level of understanding has aided in her healing.

Healing is a conscious choice. "It's hard work, but it can be done." Through self-care, Rosanne now considers herself a shining light parent rather than a bereaved one. Her first book, be*LEE*ve, *A Journey of Loss, Healing, and Hope*, was ranked number one in several categories, in both the U.S. as well as internationally.

Heaven, I Could Only Imagine
By Patricia Holgate Haney

I remember vividly as a child being curious about stories in the bible. I was fascinated with the images of Heaven and all the exotic places where events took place. I wanted to visit them all.

I was so excited to share what I read that I made little handwritten "books" going door to door in our neighborhood, selling them for ten cents each. I wanted to share the magical stories I had read.

Heaven was a recurring theme in my life.

My enthusiasm and door to door proselytizing caught the attention of neighbors who were evangelical recording artists and did revivals. When they asked if I could tour with them, not surprisingly, my parents declined. I guess I wasn't meant to go on that journey.

As a child, my grandmother and great aunt took me to the Hollywood Bowl for a holiday spectacular. I was excited to go on this memorable surprise trip, just myself and the two sisters, my Rosalind Russel-type grandmother and my glamourous great aunt. Upon arrival, we walked up a path with ethereal music coming softly from somewhere close. We turned the corner and stood gazing down upon the Bowl and seating. I then saw the colossal star and cross hanging from atop the stage and the brilliant angels holding trumpets seemingly floating above the stage.

I was going to Heaven. Why didn't they tell me I was dying? The magical place became frightening. I started whimpering, then crying louder. I stopped in my tracks, trying to break their grasp, refusing to go further.

"Patty, what is wrong?" they asked. "I don't want to die! I don't want to go to Heaven. Let's go home!" After some time spent convincing me it was a holiday production and that they most certainly weren't dropping me off in Heaven, we stayed.

Images burnt in the brain remain.

I was a sleepwalker in my youth, and my obsession with Heaven and the bible created at least one unique event. One Saturday evening before Easter, hearing some noise come from the kitchen, my parents found me in a chair pulled up to the counter, carefully dipping my white Easter shoes into the tin cups of dye used hours before to color my eggs.

"Patty, what are you doing?" "I'm getting my shoes ready to meet Jesus," I replied. According to family stories, two things saved me, my Dad's laughter at the absurdity of it and the fact that I was sleepwalking. Otherwise, I might have had a real *come to Jesus* moment.

In Sunday school, usually near the holidays, we would talk about and draw angels and other images of Heaven. Inevitably, with excited and sincere curiosity, I asked, "In the beginning, God made everyone, so who made God?" The response was consistent, with a stern look and tone, I was advised that I needed to believe, and if I couldn't, maybe I should sit there and think about it.

Yes, Heaven and religion became a puzzle for me.

At about 8 or 9, I decided that I was more interested in regular services, not in Sunday school. I wanted to learn about Heaven; I didn't want to sit and color. I never went to Sunday school again. I only went to traditional services, both in my own church and with friends and neighbors; different denominations but similar messages.

I was obsessed with sorting out the well-told stories from reality. Everywhere I looked, Heaven was a place with ethereal angels floating around and beautiful landscapes. Yet there were also those frightening images of Hell with the devil dancing among the flames and evil and scary-looking creatures.

As I got older, I was always afraid of death, of funerals, to be exact. I had not experienced any by the time my great grandmother passed. I knew I didn't want to remember her in a casket and experience, like in the movies, everyone weeping and sobbing at her death. If she was going to this place called Heaven, why the sorrow?

Over the years, I had neighbors and friends who passed, but it wasn't until losing my grandparents that I started to notice something that happened to people right before they died, right before they even knew they would.

The conversations typically revolved around their doubt of what they had accomplished, what would have happened if they had done x, y, or z?

I noticed that all had a similar set of questions they asked themselves and those around them. It seemed like they had a fear of what they had not done on earth rather than what was waiting for them in Heaven.

When my father, the genealogy expert in the family, started to talk this way, it was surprising. He was, after all, a bible scholar but genuinely agnostic. He didn't like engaging in conversations about religion, and most who knew him just accepted it. His thoughts on Heaven and death were simple—you die. Words make a lasting impression.

My father developed Parkinson's, and his personality went from a dry sense of humor and a contagious laugh to becoming more of a pessimist. As we were getting ready to find hospice care for him, he passed away. I was devastated as I felt I had failed him. He died alone. Was he afraid at the end? Did he "just die"?

After Dad was gone, my conversations with Mom became even more profound. I was blessed to have this time with Mom. Dad and I had always had a close relationship growing up, but until 20 years prior, I never really connected with Mom.

We made up for the lost time. We laughed more than we ever had, we cried together, and we talked about what we felt in our hearts. She shared thoughts and stories I'd never heard. Then it happened. Mom began saying she hadn't accomplished anything, hadn't followed some of her dreams, and had failed at some things in life.

In December of 2011, she called me saying, "Patty, I don't know why I am still here; I am just existing. I am not living."

It took my breath away. I told Mom I hate that you feel this way, but I want you to know I am glad you are here. I don't know what my day would be like without you. She replied, "Well, I love you, but *this is just not living*." Using our

134

family trait of dry humor, I replied, "Well, if you go, will you at least come back and haunt me sometimes?" She laughed and made a funny cackle sound effect saying, "Yeah, I'll come back and shake you up good." We laughed and hung up.

A few minutes later, my phone rang again, and it was Mom. She said with a soft voice, "I know I told you I'd come back and haunt you, but when I come back, I want you to know you are my angel. I am going to lay a bed of roses for you at your feet." Talking through my tears, my heart full, I said, "I'm counting on that."

Mom managed to continue residing in an independent living facility, but she was beginning to require more help. She was getting weaker. We took her to her doctor and set her up with palliative care to help keep her in her home per her wishes.

The following May, Mom's health took a turn for the worst. I called the care team, and when they came, they thought she may have about a month or two to live. I called my sisters and brother.

I recalled a few months prior, two specific instances she had shared with me. In one, Dad had come to her when she was dozing in her chair in the living room. She said he was in a cardboard box and laughing, trying to get out. Once he did, he looked at her and smiled. She felt he looked like his old self before becoming ill. "Isn't that the craziest thing?" she asked. Her other experience was one night, her mother had appeared. Mom said she was just smiling, no conversation, just smiling. When Mom tried to take her hand, Grandma told her, "Not yet, Dorrie," and disappeared.

We talked over these experiences. I asked Mom if she was afraid. "A little, but it was peaceful at the same time," she replied. She said they looked content. I asked her, do you think they were in Heaven? She replied, "I've told you, if everyone went to Heaven, it would be too crowded." We left it at that. Recalling the experience with Grandma, she said, "I guess it just wasn't my time yet, but I'd be ok if it was."

A few weeks later, Mom called, saying she couldn't move, sounding weak. When we arrived, she had managed to move to a chair at the table. She was frail, she tried to put on a cheery face, but the spark was gone from her eyes. We called the hospice team. When they arrived, they told us she did not have long. Gary and I made the decision to stay overnight in her apartment. We made a bed on the floor to stay close, not wanting her to be alone. She seemed resigned. She was, after all, as she always told us, a realist.

The next morning, when the hospice team returned, we were told she was transitioning, and they began to prepare her. Eventually, I laid next to her. She began getting morphine doses to ease her transition. She spoke quietly between sleeping. Each time she dozed off, I felt a need to tell her, "I love you, Mom" so she would not feel alone.

Her voice was altered by drugs, but she said "I love you" faintly and with difficulty. Her motor skills were fading. She opened her eyes and whispered, "You're my angel." My eyes welled with tears. The end was imminent.

The minister came. It was evident she had talked to Mom. And listened.

She brought out a recording of one of Mom's favorite songs, *Cuando Caliente el Sol*. It played in the background, softly. The door was open to her balcony and a little breeze whipped around the giant pine tree outside. The wind-chimes we had hung there began to slowly and melodically chime. The family that was able to be there spoke to her. The minister provided words of comfort. She looked peaceful. There was a slight gasp of air, then she passed.

Mom was gone.

A few months later, I was missing Mom palpably. As we drove, I asked Gary, "Did you eat an apple in the car?" He looked at me quizzically. I looked around the car, sure that I would find some fruit or something that might have fallen out of a grocery bag.

There was an intake of breath as Gary smelled it as well. It was a fragrance, sweet but light. Stopping the car, we looked at each other, and we said at almost the same time, "Roses!" It was the fragrance of roses! Could it be? Was it real? Gary and I both got tears in our eyes, but also big smiles on our faces. She knew we needed her. She brought me my sign. She had brought the roses as promised.

This was my answer regarding Heaven. Mom sent me a message that day, one I will never forget. My journey to find an answer may have taken a long time, but I stopped thinking that Heaven was a place. I quit worrying about Heaven and Hell's images.

For me, it became a feeling. A realization. A blessing. I felt a sense of peace. With her indomitable spirit, Doris M. Holgate, and her ability to rise above any situation with a positive attitude gave me a gift. I finally knew Heaven. Thank you with love.

Bio

Patricia Holgate Haney is a travel professional and author after a career in corporate management in both the for-profit and nonprofit sectors. An avid traveler, she volunteers with organizations dedicated to helping the underserved. She believes that love is a never-ending circle that brings us all together and that Love, Kindness and Gratitude make the world a better place. Married to her soul mate, Gary, Mother of Kevin and Josh, Grandmother and Great Grandmother family is her treasure. Website: phtravels.com, email: pholgatehaney@gmail.com.

Forty-Eight Hours
By Marianne Hudspeth

11/17/2020

Two hours ago, I hit an old man with my car. Maybe he hit me, I'm not sure. He was driving a golf cart in Sun City West, AZ. It's not unusual to see older people in golf carts, as they use them for basic transportation.

I was on my way to an appointment with a new physician, a pulmonologist, and I wasn't sure where his office was located. I found the building and, after signaling, turned right to enter the parking lot. I heard the crash before I saw the old man who was driving his golf cart on the right side of my car. I saw his hand and arm grabbing for the air when he flew out of his golf cart onto the hard driveway into the parking lot. It was all in slow motion, like when you're dreaming and have to run through cement.

As I got out of my car, I saw him lying on his left side and asked him if I should call 911. "Are you okay? Did you hit your head on the curb?"

"Yes. Call them," he said. He didn't move much but seemed alert and oriented. A lady approached me from behind and asked me if I was okay because I was shaking and very concerned about the man on the ground. I felt her reassuring hand lightly rubbing my back like a mother would do when her child is inconsolable. I ran back to my car to turn the hazard lights on and grabbed a mask. Because, you know, Covid-19.

The sheriff's department arrived right after the ambulance. A few people had helped the man to his feet. I remember saying, "I don't think he should try to stand before the paramedics get here," but he stood up anyway. When the paramedics arrived, they said he seemed okay but took him to "get checked out anyway, just in case."

I moved my car to a parking space because it was still in the driveway of the parking lot.

The deputy asked me where I was headed when the accident happened. I told him I was on my way to the pulmonologist's appointment. He asked me if I wanted to go check-in for the appointment. I thought in my mental and sweaty condition that may be a good idea, so I walked up the block, still crying, and gave the receptionist my papers to register and told her that I had just been in a traffic accident, and she offered to reschedule. I rescheduled for the next day.

The deputy was still writing his report when I got back to my car. He was very kind and asked me how I was feeling, and he took my statement. I burst into tears and told him that I was a nurse, and I don't hurt people; I help them. He was very supportive, saying, "That's why these things are called 'accidents.'"

So then, out of nowhere, like a waking dream or calming presence, a peaceful, calm feeling came over me, like a warming blanket, and something shifted in me. I thought about the turmoil in this country and how painful and divided and raggedy everyone seems right now. And I looked around me and saw lovely, concerned, caring, nurturing people all around me. Nobody asked me for whom I voted. Nobody screamed at me or purposely coughed in my face. Nearly everyone had a mask on, and I saw love. I saw caring people helping others like I haven't seen in a long time.

Maybe I have not been trying to see it hard enough.

Just like Mr. Roger's mom said, I looked for and saw the helpers.

And they are here, these folks, young and old, male and female, democrats and republicans and independents, all colors of the rainbow and people of every stripe were there to help in this messy, traumatic time. I was so astonished and happy to see them all together in one place, cooperating (you call 911, and I'll pick up the broken glass?) by just being humans on the earth.

Everyone was showing their love and their humanity. I felt so much hope at that moment. It made me understand, like I haven't in a long time, that we will be okay.

This seems to me like extraordinary oneness.

Now it's the next day.

I just heard from my dear friend, Karen. She is a fellow nurse who currently works as a school nurse in this time of covid-19 craziness. I worry about her every day because of this, but I also know that if anyone can handle the responsibility of caring for elementary kids and staff, it's going to be super-smart, super-organized Karen.

We have been close friends since we met at church camp when our kids were in first grade. I was acting as the camp nurse because that was the only way I could afford to send my two boys to camp. She was acting as a camp counselor. She was the counselor for the group, which included one of my boys. He is black and adopted from Haiti. They were giving each other nicknames for the week, and she asked my son what nickname he would like. He said, "Cookie because I'm like an Oreo, black on the outside and white on the inside." That's when Karen decided, "I gotta meet this kid's mother." We have been close friends since that day. Those kids are now close to forty years old.

Karen had surgery on her thumb yesterday and is recovering at home.

Today, she told me that her Mom is in hospice, actively dying from Covid-19. She cannot visit her because of her immediate post-surgical status, but her RN daughter, Carrie, can. Karen is waiting to hear from her daughter as I write this.

There isn't much I can offer my friend at this moment, but to be available by phone to comfort her when she is ready and just be present for her, long distance. We call each other to cry in life's horrible and shitty times, help each other to not be so terrified in this general craziness, and usually, we end laughing, the kind of laughter that puts us at serious risk of peeing ourselves. We celebrate happy times like crazy because you never know when it's your last page in your book.

She lost her dad in 2018. She lost her sister almost exactly one year ago. Her mom looks to be teetering on the edge between here and there. Now it's my turn to be her safe place until the clench is gone for her. She and I agree that our creed is mostly "Don't be an asshole, and do not hang with assholes."

And, as Ram Dass said, "We're all just walking each other home."

Even though she lives in Illinois and I live in Arizona, we know that we can connect anytime.

She loves to make exquisite quilts. It's her art form. She told me that when she makes a quilt for one of her people, she thinks about that person the whole time she is making it. I love that. She has made a beautiful quilt for me twice. Those quilts have medicinal powers, like roses or a warm cup of tea with lemon and honey.

I just got a text from her that read, 'Mom just went to heaven.'

So now my heart is screaming, 'Call her right now!' My better angels are saying, 'Give her space, and she will receive the grace.'

That's nice. If I were in charge of how things in life work, I wouldn't even put that on a bumper sticker. But I'm not in charge of good ideas. It's all a mess up there in my head. My mind is crowded with continuous random crap.

I had to have a procedure recently in the cardiac catheterization lab, and my mouth would just not stop talking. I remember saying, "God, I hope I don't swear too f--king much." Then I remember everyone laughing. The anesthesia person said that she thought maybe I needed more drugs than the average bear, like a tranquilizer dart. My reply was, "You should watch me try to go to sleep every night."

I read my kindle with the night setting turned on. I listen to music and meditation recordings. I meditate for about 20 seconds until I can hear my head laughing at me, saying things like 'nice try, crazy one.' I pray too, but this is usually interrupted by my mind wondering about things like 'did I turn all the ceiling fans off? What should I take out of the freezer for dinner tomorrow?' You know, real earth-shattering things like that can continue for an hour or so.

I know: ADD, ADHD. I had meds that I took *one time* for that. Adderall makes me even crazier than normal. So sometimes, when I'm still awake at 4 AM, I just think, 'Oh well, I'll just sleep until noon.' See? Even now, I'm getting distracted by myself.

So I have to try to give myself some rules for bringing me back to 'normal.'

I cannot watch the news. I'm pretty strict with myself because I can go from feeling good and having hope for the country and myself to a dark place in a cave of despair in the time it takes to watch the news. I have cut anything political from my Facebook feed, and if a troll or a bad meme shows up, I have to unfollow the person who posted this crap or just hide the comments. This mostly works for me. I have unfollowed family members and some actual friends.

But when I'm my craziest self, the one thing that brings me back to my slightly less crazy self is my motorcycle. It's a Harley-Davidson Sportster low riding touring model. I have had many different bikes, but this one is the first one that physically fits me.

When I get in the wind on my bike, I feel free in just the right amount of time. Not too quickly because if I just shrug stuff off, it doesn't process, and then it comes right back. If I 'dwell on' stuff, it just gets worse. The wind makes me feel free and cleansed, like bed sheets that have been dried on the clothesline of my youth. When I smell the clean wind, I feel lighter and stronger. Invincible almost. Like I'm flying free from gravity's force.

Sometimes I ride out on the 303 south and turn west on Bell Road. This takes me out in the desert where there is very little traffic, past the housing developments. Then I stop, turn off the bike and just look at the beauty in the wild and ground myself. Cacti, mountains, roadrunners, bunnies, and quiet. The vastness of the blue sky tells me that there is so much more to this than the things that hijack our attention. This helps me appreciate what has been given to us here on this beautiful blue marble. I drink a bottle of water and visualize how it is cleaning all that grit and grime that life sneaks in there and clogs up the works.

If I listen, I hear, deep in my soul, the message that everything will always be alright.

Bio

Marianne is a published author, Naturopathic Physician, Registered Nurse, Reiki Master, Observer/tester for ATD (therapy dogs), and has organized several medical mission trips to Haiti to deliver healthcare. Her passions include being a helper in the world and a fierce lover of justice and peace. She rides her own Harley-Davidson Sportster Touring motorcycle and loves spreading love through humor. She is a self-proclaimed bad-ass. She lives in Arizona with her beloved and retired (God help her) husband, Jim.

The Sacred in the Ordinary
By Rosemary Hurwitz

I remember the first time I heard "the sacred in the ordinary." It was articulated more specifically, and it felt like an insightful commandment.

"Find the sacred in the ordinary," said John Shea, Theologian and Author, who was enlightening us on a windy Sunday at Loyola University. I remember feeling like I was going to learn something meaningful that day.

His words spoke to me and brought new meaning to what ordinary is and how it is a part of all of us. It continues to speak to me fifteen years later.

What does "find the sacred in the ordinary" mean? Does it mean that we find joy in little things or in average things, or even in the mundane things, or is it deeper than that? Is sacred a state of mind too, or do we feel sacred? What is meant by sacred? The definition of sacred is "connected with God," or "holy," or as I like to spell it, whole-y, meaning our whole-ness.

It feels like an appropriate time to write this essay. It is a grey day, an ordinary weekday. It is a few days after Christmas when most of the celebrating world feels its fatigue after a month (at least) of giving and trying to stand out and be anything but ordinary. No, we would like to feel special, like the Little Drummer Boy of the famed song. At this time of year especially, we long to show our Christ-light, no matter our tradition of faith or the absence of it.

We want to be some kind of beacon, to someone or to many, who mean so much to us. We may even envy those who are like cream that rises to the top in some way. After all of our energy is put out there, and when we feel done and the holiday is over, we can get that letdown feeling. That "after vacation blues" feeling. The special holiday time is over, or is it?

There is a children's story in which a little boy wonders why every day cannot be as extraordinary as Christmas. His mom goes through all the details of preparing for the Christmas season and shows why with all that goes into the special time, it can only be just once a year. She impresses upon him the more important message of Christmas. Keeping Christmas in your heart all year, she tells him, means shining your light bigger and loving others as you do yourself, even more, each day. That is the real meaning of Christmas. To work at being and doing your best is the goal of every day, not just at Christmastime. To know and act from the belief that all of us are extraordinary beings created in the image of our Divine Source. A great lesson for children and adults alike.

After the holidays are over, the feeling of being ordinary again can seep in after a season of heightened inner awareness and great energy that extends outward. Time to resolve to make the new year better, time for resolutions that help us to be anything but our ordinary selves. For most of us, resolution-makers or not, this is a real feeling of a letdown, and romantics can feel it and take it the hardest.

The good news is often with a little rest, and self-acceptance we uncover that deepened awareness that we need.

Compassion for both our self and other loved ones graces, centers, and reenergizes us. This grace is always within us, ready to be delivered like a package from Amazon on our doorstep. With attention, reflection and intention, it is ours for the taking. In moments of stress and fatigue, it just feels absent, and we lose our balance. Disconnected from our divinity, we are not enough, we are not special, we are abandoned, we are ordinary, we are victims. We are human.

After a letdown of any kind, or just a "bad" day, with honest reflection, we realize we were the ones who disconnected from our essential self. The insights and grace are always there for the taking, but it is always a process to get there. The inner work is worth it because when we do it, we know from a deep place that our loved ones and ourselves are anything but ordinary. We realize we are a both/and of shining and grime, of specialness and ordinary, of unique and alike and of energy and fatigue. We are just a both/and of so many things, and this realization feels wonderful! It is the human process. It is how growth occurs. This self-acceptance is how Christmas can occur every day as we feel a part of the *one* divine light and move through letdowns, disappointments, failures, and feeling ordinary.

Our ordinary oneness is simply being and sharing what ordinary or human looks like. We can share the pain of being ordinary when we want to be more, and we can share the joy in being ordinary when we feel we are enough. It is all good. Our feelings are what bond us to each other. We are all different and the same, different in our unique personalities and the same in that we are human. If we are human, we are both ordinary and sacred, human and divine, or connected with (part of) God.

As a long time teacher of the Enneagram, which is a holistic system for understanding the nine universal personality types and its purpose to connect our personality to our unique essence more deeply, I would like to share how 'Finding the sacred in the ordinary" is key inner work for The Romantic, also called The Original or Individualist on the Enneagram.

While it is a great phrase to reflect on no matter your personality type, it is especially the personal growth path of Type Four, The Original Romantic. This type has a blind spot or area of avoidance, and it is "ordinary or common." He avoids the ordinary because he perceived it as a shortcoming, a weakness in himself and others.

How does "find the sacred in the ordinary" then apply to The Individualist? Their emotional passion or driving energy is longing. They long to be special and may envy those who seem better than they are. They long to rise above, to stand out, to shine brighter. They do this because of a perceived or real abandonment in their childhood.

Particularly in stressful situations, the Individualist believes if they stand out, they will be better loved. However, their inner spiritual work is to know that their abandonment wound can be healed. Their story of trying so hard to be special to gain the attention of the one who abandoned them no longer needs to be so central. With deepened awareness and Enneagram wisdom, their pattern of avoiding ordinary behaviors as a way to be special, gain approval, and attention no longer dominates their persona.

With a deeper awareness and knowing that we are all a part of the divine *oneness*, they can heal and feel this ordinary oneness. They no longer need to long to be "readmitted to the garden of Eden," as Enneagram Author Jerome Wagner writes, because they know they have never "been expelled from it."

With this sacred insight, there is healing, and their blind spot of avoiding the ordinary is no longer in the dark for them. In stress, it will arise within for them, but with this new self-awareness, they can name it, embrace it and its lessons and navigate through it much better.

In other words, they do not have to try so hard to be extraordinary because they are loved and belong, all of the time. Their old story of not being enough, of being common and ordinary, in the eyes of their important parent or caregiver who they felt less loved by, can fade and lose its grip.

We can learn so much from this personality type and all of the nine types on the Enneagram. Emotional wellness and spiritual connection go hand in hand because we are safe, loved and enough when we are in God's love and light.

Ordinary oneness is a sacred state of being with our human pain. It is the process of our deepening connection to our God-Source that we come from. It is in cultivating our compassion for ourselves and others that we realize our connection to each other. It is here we know our divine and ordinary oneness.

Bio

Rosemary Hurwitz is passionate about an inner-directed life, and she found the focus for it in the Enneagram, a personality to higher consciousness paradigm respected and practiced worldwide. Since her Certification in 2001, she has studied, taught and coached for self-awareness and emotional wellness, with the Enneagram and the intuitive process. She is an Accredited Professional Member of the International Enneagram Association. Rosemary teaches at The Theosophical Society of America, The Present Moment, Be Optimal, Common Ground, and others in Chicago and virtually. She has been published in ten inspirational anthologies and the latest, *The Courageous Heart, Finding Strength in Difficult Times*. Her first single-authored, Amazon bestselling book is *Who You Are Meant to Be: The Enneagram Effect*.

Connect with Rosemary at www.spiritdrivenliving.com. www.Facebook.com/rosemaryhurwitz, www.instagram.com/enneagram_empowerment, www.twitter.com@rosemaryhurwitz, www.linkedin.com/rosemaryhurwitz

Who Do You Think I Am?
By Cindy J. Kaufman, MEd, EdS

T he answer to that will probably depend on what labels you use to define me.

When I lived in the city of Denver years ago, there was a man who stood on the corner, one block away from my house and, nearly all day, every day there he would be, holding a sign asking passing motorists for financial assistance when they stopped for the red light. When I took walks in the neighborhood, sometimes I would walk in his direction and greet him with a "hello," as I crossed the intersection. He would say hello back to me, and sometimes we would make small talk if I had to wait for the red light to cross the street.

One day, as I walked toward "the homeless guy on the corner," he smiled and announced gleefully, "Today is my birthday!" "Well, happy birthday to you," I offered to him as I stopped for the red light. "Guess how old I am today," he said to me. "I have no idea," I responded, "How old are you today?" "I'm 67," he replied, "67 years old." I was glad I had not guessed his age because he looked much older than 67 to me! As the light turned green, I again wished him a happy birthday as I walked away. In the middle of the intersection, I turned back and gave him a smile and a wave as I continued across the street. I wished I'd had something more I could give him for his birthday.

The next day I put a $20 bill in my pocket when I went on my walk, and I gave him a belated birthday present, for which he seemed incredibly grateful and asked if he could shake my hand. "Of course," I responded and extended my hand to him. Whenever I spoke about him to someone else, if I were to share an experience or conversation we had, I would refer to him as "the homeless guy on the corner." Rather than bothering to ask his name, I gave him a label.

My encounters with "the homeless guy on the corner" became more frequent when I became the caretaker for my daughter's two small dogs. The dogs required daily walks, so I would often head in the direction of "the homeless guy on the corner." He always seemed happy to see the dogs coming toward him, and he began referring to them as "Salt and Pepper" because one was white and the other was black. "Here come Salt and Pepper!" he would loudly exclaim with a smile as we walked toward him. We would quite often exchange small talk by this point in time, especially about the dogs, as we saw each other with more regularity.

One day, as I looked out of my living room window, I saw "the homeless guy on the corner" walking down my street. He turned and went between two buildings across the street from my apartment. The next day when I went for my walk, I took a look down between those two buildings. I realized that this is where he was living. He had a little camp with a lean-to set up in the back between the buildings. I had this "A-ha!" moment. He wasn't "the homeless guy on the corner." He was my neighbor. We lived on the same street. We coexisted on the same block. It didn't matter that I had a roof and four walls and he had a lean-to, or that I made money working at a university while he made money asking others for it at a traffic light. We were neighbors just like every other neighbor who lived on my street.

Once I had this perspective, I began to see him differently. The next time I went for a walk, I approached him, just like any other day, but I made sure it wasn't any other day. I stopped and said, "You know, I've been passing by and chatting with you almost every day for a long time, and I want to apologize. I've never asked your name." He smiled his same sweet smile and said, "My name is Robert." "Robert," I said, "I'm Cindy. It's nice to meet you." "It's nice to meet you," he responded. And from that day on, I said, "Hello, Robert," when I passed him on the street, and he replied, "Hello, Cindy." And I stopped referring to him as "the homeless guy on the corner." If I spoke about him, I used his name. I felt we had become friends. In a neighborhood that didn't always feel safe to walk in, I believed Robert was someone who would look out for me if I was ever in trouble. Fortunately, I never needed his help.

We eventually moved away from that neighborhood, and I never saw my friend Robert again. Robert taught me something significant. I no longer look at someone on the street without seeing them first and foremost as a human being and seeing their circumstances as separate from the person, not a label by which to identify them.

The point of this story is to demonstrate one of the problems with "labels." As long as I referred to Robert as "the homeless guy on the corner," I dehumanized him. Calling him that made him no more significant than "the light pole on the corner." I had effectively reduced him down to the smallness of my label for him. He was a thing, an object. I was never outwardly unkind to Robert in any of my interactions with him, but the label I had given him felt like an unkind characterization of him to others.

To refer to him as the "homeless guy on the corner" emphasized our differences, deemphasized any similarities, allowed me to ignore him as a human being, and failed to give him the consideration and respect he deserved. Because I had a limited impression of him didn't mean he wasn't worth more, or that he was worthless. Was the label untrue? No. Robert was, in fact, a homeless guy on the corner, but he was more than that. When I consider how genuinely kind he was, and how positive and happy he always seemed to be, despite any hardships he had, I had used a label that devalued him for far too long and, for that, I am deeply sorry.

Labels can devalue people, turn them into "other," and serve to separate us. They also allow us to believe, "You are that, and I am not that." As long as people are "other," as long as we emphasize our differences, as long as we believe a person's circumstances define them, and as long as we fail to give a person consideration, we keep them insignificant. And if we see people as less than, we will treat them as such. For instance, using the label "immigrant," or worse, "illegal immigrant," to describe a person, a human being, who comes to this country in search of a better life, or for the sanctuary to escape harm or harmful threats, serves to make them an "other." We label them by their circumstance, without any regard for the individual, their experiences, or the situation that forced them into making life-altering or life-saving decisions.

One place that labels have become particularly troublesome is in politics. The political divisions have become so toxic in our country. The political labels we use to describe people have become so demonized. It is no wonder we have such a great divide that seems to be ever-deepening to the detriment of this country.

Regardless of any labels put upon a person, or their political leanings, their beliefs, or who gets their vote, there is not one label that defines a person in totality. Also, they often imply that a person is an enemy based solely on that alone. The labels Republican, Democrat, conservative, liberal, right, left, red, or blue are all terms that have become synonymous with "other." Not only that, they have become charged with negative emotions, causing us to dislike, or to hate, anyone whose label is not our own based exclusively on that label. They help us categorize the world, but not always in helpful ways.

There are labeling theories in psychology, sociology, criminology, and other sciences that will not be given justice in this chapter. It was not my intent to talk academically about the in-depth research on how labels affect self-esteem, how they impact our behaviors, or how they affect entire societies of people. No, this was not my focus here. My intent here is more pragmatic, more helpful. Think before you judge another person solely based on one or two labels that you believe explain who they are and who they are not. Think about the myriad of labels that people use. They are truly endless in categories. We label people about politics, religion, ethnicity, race, age, gender, sexual preference, career, hobbies, the state in which a person lives, or the country in which a person was born, to name a few.

In reality, labels say so little about a person. They make everything black and white when there is, in actuality, so much gray in the world and people, as far as the way they think, believe, and behave. Labels pigeonhole people into superficial and misleading characterizations, and they prevent us from exploring beyond the surface, leaving us knowing little to nothing about a person based solely on a label. If it keeps us from sitting down with a person to have a conversation and getting to know them, then it prevents interactions and relationships we might otherwise have had.

People are more alike than they are different. We all coexist in the same world, each of us a part of that which makes up the whole. Rather than focusing on the "you-ness" and the "me-ness" that keeps us separated, we could focus on the "one-ness." If we looked past the labels to the ordinary likeness that we have in common, that brings us together, rather than what disconnects us, how might our world be different?

I work with people at the end of their lives as an end-of-life doula. I've been doing end-of-life work, sitting at the bedside having conversations with the dying, for many years. One thing that I have learned is that at the end of our lives, most of the things we've concerned ourselves with while we are living are not the things we find ourselves caring about at the end of our lives. The ego mainly falls away, and people become their most real and their most authentic selves when they know their time on earth is limited. All those labels we use to define and separate ourselves from others mean absolutely nothing in the end. It is our oneness we find ourselves embracing. The connections we feel to others are some of the most valued of life's gifts, but sometimes we are not aware of this until the end. We may realize that we've limited or perhaps lost connections with others because of the way we judged them based on some preconceived notion we had about who they are because of a label we used to define them. It is the relationship we have with others that we think about when our time is limited. The connections, the oneness we feel, will be what matters to us the most when all the labels fall away.

Bio

Cindy J. Kaufman, MEd, EdS, brings her background in counselor education, as well as her more than 25 years as a hospice volunteer, to her work as a Certified End of Life Doula, home funeral guide, death educator, and author of the international best-selling book, *The Mortal's Guide to Dying Well: Practical Wisdom from an End of Life Doula.* Cindy is the owner of HeartSpeak End of Life Companioning LLC, and she is President of the Colorado End-of-Life Collaborative. She serves as a compassionate companion on life's final journey for the dying person and their loved ones. In addition, Cindy is an ordained interfaith minister and is trained in home funerals and green burials, and she can guide clients who want these options. Cindy is based in Denver, Colorado, and can be reached at cindy@heartspeak2u.com or www.heartspeak2u.com.

Walks with Oz
By Donna Kiel

arly morning, the day after Thanksgiving, during a global pandemic, I was annoyed that Ozzie, my eleven-year-old black lab, wouldn't go outside. I was tired and had the effects of post-Thanksgiving overeating. For me, that includes feeling guilty, bloated, and annoyed with whoever made me eat as if there was no tomorrow. Ozzie deciding not to get up was just another annoying factor in my post-holiday pandemic angst. After about an hour, the annoyance slowly turned to concern. What is going on with him? A very food-motivated being, much like me, I tried the offering of treats. Nothing. I tried the reliable method of showing him his leash to go for a walk. Nothing. My frustration grew.

A symptom of the pandemic permeating my life was a quick, intense response of anger to anything. Pandemic life had become overwhelming to me. My days of never-ending Zoom meetings and a workload that shockingly increased rather than decreased were too much. Pre-pandemic, I spent my days with hour-long commutes to the university where I am faculty and to schools where I lead workshops for teachers. I was in constant motion leaving home at 6:00 a.m. and returning long after 7:00 p.m. Two days a week, I watch my toddler granddaughter and fit in work during her nap time. My life pre-pandemic was beyond hectic. I often dreamed of just staying in one place.

The pandemic stay-at-home order was welcome to me. As an introvert and an exhausted professional, I imagined my life slowing down. I thought the pandemic would give me time to write, rest, gain insight, and do the things I wanted. The pivot to remote teaching was easy for me. I liked teaching online. What I didn't anticipate was my own insecurity surfacing and that I would take on the role of passionate rescuer. It was as if my response to the pandemic was to grab my superhero cape and become the savior of every elementary and high school teacher forced into remote teaching. Then in May of 2020, when we awakened to systemic racism, that cape of mine got bigger. I joined with three incredible African American women to train teachers on how to integrate racial equity in the remote school experience. My days went from constant motion and busyness to exhaustive hours of engaging in virtual Zoom meetings.

The day after Thanksgiving, all I wanted was downtime. Ozzie's episode caused me to snap. It was that proverbial straw for a camel whose back was already broken. Just as I was about to rage, Ozzie was up and wanting to go out. Great! It was done. Ozzie went outside and took care of his bodily functions, and laid down outside on the ground.

It was about 50 degrees outside and not too cold for a dog with a fur coat. After about an hour, Ozzie hadn't moved from where he laid down. Attempts to get him to come in were useless. He wasn't moving. After another two hours, Ozzie still wasn't moving. Now, he was breathing short, shallow, quick breaths and just staring off into the distance. His beautiful black eyes had lost that welcoming glance I came to count on.

Ozzie and I have an interesting relationship. He isn't even my dog. Eleven years ago, my daughter brought Ozzie home for her dad. Ozzie is a rambunctious, playful, strong, and large dog. I have always been a small dog type of person. I like to be able to pick up a pet and cuddle close. Ozzie is not a cuddly little bundle of fur. Ozzie is 110 pounds of playfulness. His strength often frustrated me. When I came home, he was so excited he would jump like a kangaroo, grab a shoe, and then jump up on me. For Ozzie's entire life, my typical words to him were "stop it."

Yet, Ozzie seemed to know me better than I knew myself. Years earlier, as I struggled to deal with losing a job I had poured myself into and then losing a cherished Carin Terrier named Dusty, Ozzie broke through the boundaries I had established in our relationship and comforted me. The night after my beloved Carin Terrier, Dusty died, Ozzie jumped up on my bed and laid on my feet. Granted, his presence on the bed was physically crushing, but it was the comfort and connection that allowed me to grieve with safety. I loved Ozzie, and I also resisted Ozzie's over-whelming attention. He was my buddy and a royal pain in the ass. Our relationship was as complex as my under-standing of me.

As I went outside to check on Ozzie, his eyes were vacant. He was dying. I knew that breath. That familiar sound of life leaving a body. I told family members they should go out and say goodbye. No matter what I tried, I couldn't get him to get up and come inside.

I searched for a mobile vet, thinking that perhaps he needed to have his suffering ended. It was cold, he was lying in a bed of gravel, and it was breaking my heart. I hugged him and gently thanked him for the love he gave me. I whispered to him that I loved him and that he had saved my broken heart, and I was forever grateful. I told him it was okay for him to go, and he would always be with me. As someone who always holds tightly onto anything—from a work routine to a loved one and now to Ozzie, I knew I needed to let go. Letting go would free Ozzie and free me.

I've learned the importance of letting go. In my studies of philosophy and psychology, I've learned the ancient wisdom teachings that letting go of attachment to anything is the pathway to true happiness. I've studied all the masters from Carl Jung to Laozi. The words and message are always the same. If you want to ease your suffering, if you want to get closer to living your most authentic life, you must let go. Letting go is a challenge for me. Letting go is such a challenge that I even cringe when I hear the song "Let it Go" from the Disney movie *Frozen*. Letting go is painful. Yet, letting go has always served me well. I'm not sure why I continue to fight to let go.

When I let go of Dusty, I opened the way for seeing my strength and resiliency. When I let go of the professional title of principal, which I believed defined me, I opened the door to the happiness of being a creative writer and teacher. When I let go of the pain of not having the love I longed for from my mother and father, I opened my heart to become a playful and unconditionally loving grandmother. I had learned the power of letting go, but the process of doing it was a beast. Now, I knew I had to let go of Ozzie. He wouldn't respond. He had been outside for six hours.

I finally found a mobile vet. He looked at Ozzie and had us slip the towel around under his belly and make a sling. He then told us to pull him up. Ozzie struggled, and I felt like I couldn't breathe. Seeing Ozzie's pain was unbearable.

The vet gave Ozzie a pain shot. I asked him if Ozzie was dying. My question seemed to surprise him. He didn't seem to know that letting go is what we are supposed to do. He said he needed to take blood and see what was going on.

He directed me to give Ozzie the meds in a few hours and let the injection take effect. The vet left, and I was convinced I spent $500.00 to get Ozzie from the back yard to the house to die. I convinced the family it was time to say goodbye. Then, my daughter came to the house. As she entered, all of a sudden, Ozzie was walking toward her. He was wagging his tail, a bit more calmly than typical, but he was up. What was going on? Ozzie was up and moving. It's hard to let go of my attachment to Ozzie if he is now up and moving.

The great Dominican mystic Meister Eckhart (1260–1328) said, "God is not found in the soul by adding anything, but by a process of subtraction." In a flash of insight, I realized it wasn't letting go of Ozzie that I needed to do, but it was letting go of the feelings of frustration and discontent I had with Ozzie wanting my attention. I was holding tight to the belief that work was more important than spending hours talking to a black lab lying on the ground. What happened next may seem a little woo-woo or insane, but it is the learning of my lifetime.

I felt pulled to text a friend who is an Emotional Freedom Technique (tapping) coach. She had mentioned a healing method that she had used to heal pets. She had given me cotton that held the energy of the healing. I texted her and told her about Ozzie. She asked me to text her a picture of him. She directed me to put the cotton under Ozzie.

The moment Ozzie walked to my daughter, it felt as if my entire life changed. From work-obsessed, exhausted, and divided, I became clear, calm, and focused on healing Ozzie and learning from him. I didn't need to let go; I needed to hold tight to that which matters most—to the calling of my heart to be present, to be alive, and to connect—even if connecting was to a black lab.

As I write this, now nearly a month after I believed Ozzie was dying, the magical Oz continues to save my soul each day. My days of endless Zoom meetings have not stopped but what has stopped is my resistance to connecting with Ozzie or those I love. Each day, I take this magical Oz for a walk, and as I hold tight to his leash, I ask him what message he has for me. Inevitable, I hear a whisper of "you are loved" and "trust that you will know."

Now, when I spend hours at my laptop, Oz nudges my fingers off the keys. He follows me from room to room to remind me to do less work and instead to connect with my soul by taking him for a walk in the quiet.

For as long as I can remember, I have been studying and trying to prove my life is worthwhile. I've believed that my value on this earth is the work I do for others. Granted, the work I do has brought me an income and great affirmation. It took holding tight to the wonderful Oz's leash for me to realize that I am not that work but rather that I am born to connect.

I'm not sure what happened to Ozzie or if he will be with me much longer. What I do know is that I feel like I am finally home in my own life. The wonderful Oz offered me a lifeline (or leash) to hold tight. I didn't need decades of self-help books, psychology, my doctoral degree or constant professional achievements. Ozzie showed me I needed to stop the work and take walks in the quiet to hear the calling of my soul. If you are searching, wanting that oneness of your soul, take a lesson from the wonderful Oz and stop. Stop doing and instead hold tight to silence and take a walk. After, you'll get a treat—the treat will be the life you've always longed for.

Bio

Donna Kiel is a thought leader, wisdom teacher, change maker and a guide for those seeking their best life. Donna has a unique ability to inspire you to discover and live your highest potential. Donna's expertise, training, and engaging and welcoming style provide the compassion and connection needed to discover your own genius and passion. Donna is a coach, mentor, best-selling author, professor, and architect of change who works for equity and empathy in every context. Donna holds a doctorate in educational leadership and is a certified counselor and trained life coach. Donna created the empathy framework with practical tools to lead individuals and organizations to experience new levels of connection, creativity, and success. Donna is often sought for innovative change efforts by organizations and individuals seeking solutions to systemic and life challenges. Donna inspires, enlivens, and creates useful and practical solutions. Donna is the epitome of inspiration and integrity for those seeking meaning, insight, and concrete answers to the next steps in life. Donna is currently a professor, speaker, coach, and mentor offering workshops, individual coaching, anxiety relief, career planning, and life mapping sessions. She can be reached at drdonnakiel@gmail.com or through her website at https://donnakiel.com.

The Day the Jaybird Came
Over to Play
By Amy I. King

"Hope springs eternal" from the Alexander Pope poem An Essay on Man is a saying that my mom often used as I grew up.

We always have hope. I believe that it is sometimes all that we have when everything else has been exhausted. "You have cancer in your left breast," I heard as I was lying in the sunshine of the toasty July day. It was a voice so clear that it was as if someone were sitting beside me in conversation. In the summer, it was my routine to get outside for at least a 30-minute meditation. I thought to myself, what was that? I disregarded it and went on with my day. I know that sounds insane, but I had heard the voice many times throughout my life. A connection to the universe, which is the epitome of ordinary oneness, I have always considered a gift. This time I thought I just imagined things.

A few weeks later, in early September, my sister had a mammogram and had been called in for additional testing. Her biopsy came back clear. At the very end of October, I decided it was time to get mine. I went in, thinking to myself, it's just a routine mammogram. Well, I was wrong! That voice had been trying to warn me. About five days after my mammogram, I received a call to come back for further testing. I went in the following week for a second

168

mammogram, followed immediately that day by an ultrasound, and ultimately biopsies on both sides. I was at the hospital alone through it all. I was shaking uncontrollably during the biopsies. One of the nurses held my hand the entire time to make me feel less alone.

A few days later, I received the phone call no one wants. The doctor said, "The right breast is fine, but there's cancer in the left breast. My heart dropped into my stomach, and I began to cry into the phone. I sat alone, crying for a while, and then I started making calls. The entire experience was surreal to me. I felt like I was a bystander watching everything happen. I am no stranger to challenges, but I thought that I had had my share and didn't need cancer on top of all of the other challenges I had faced. I had been born with Spina bifida, a neural tube defect. My entire family, sans my sister and her family, had passed in the ten years previous to my diagnosis. Additionally, I had spent almost a year in a hospital bed in 2011. Why? Victim mode was setting in, but I quickly turned myself around and decided that facing this head-on was best. After all, that is precisely how I had handled everything I had encountered up until then.

That August, I had met and started developing a friendship with Jonathan. He happens to be a naturopath. I feel as though our meeting was divine intervention. He assured me that everything would be fine. He had my back and was going to make sure that I would be just fine. It was a serendipitous meeting for which I am grateful and another example of the oneness of it all. The universe does step in to provide us with everything and everyone we need at any given time.

I spoke to one of my best friends, Tommy, who invited me to book a flight and spend Thanksgiving with him and his husband instead of home alone. Thanksgiving at his house is always a huge affair. About 30 guests and tons of fun. I immediately said yes, and a couple of weeks later was on a flight.

My friend John, Tommy's roommate at the time, was losing his battle to cancer. He had it previously, and it had come back. Another example of oneness, He was ending his cancer journey, and I was starting mine. However, neither of us ever uttered the word cancer during that entire 5-day visit. We sat and talked for hours. We talked about his time working for Joan Rivers. He told me stories about the famous people he had met and the fun he had. We laughed and joked and talked about the serious stuff. He gave me a few of his valued possessions, some of his photos of the famous people he had interviewed, and his mother's favorite bracelet. I wear that bracelet when I am missing him most. I left Palm Springs feeling safe and loved. Tommy feels like home to me. He is always the first person I turn to when I need comfort.

Back to the reality of my situation, a male surgeon had been assigned to my case. I asked my sister, who has connections to many medical professionals, to ask around. She received a recommendation for a female doctor, which was my preference, in this case, as men don't have breasts and cannot understand what a woman goes through when dealing with breast surgery.

Because I need my arms for independence, I would have a lumpectomy without removing lymph nodes. The concern was that if they take lymph nodes, I may not be able to use my left arm should lymphodema be an issue.

I chose to wait until right after Christmas to have the surgery. The surgeon was comfortable with my decision as the type of cancer I had was slow-growing. I realize that most people would choose to have surgery as soon as possible. However, I didn't want to ruin anyone's Christmas, and I trusted my intuition.

Johnathan (the naturopath) and I created a plan. Having a plan of attack gave me hope that everything would be alright. I would have the lumpectomy followed by the treatments that were determined by my hair and saliva samples. I researched diet, removing anything harmful from my kitchen. I started using cast iron skillets for cooking instead of the coated nonstick pans. Bathroom products were analyzed and discarded, as well. I put my focus on what I could do to change what I was putting into my body. I was going to do this my way, no radiation. No judgment if you have gone the radiation route, it just didn't feel right to me.

After surgery, I began taking naturopathic medicines. I had to set the alarm for every 4 hours, waking in the middle of the night to take medications. It was not easy, but after a while, I got used to it. And even better, I began to feel healthier and happier. I loved myself in such an intense way for the first time in my life. I had a regimented routine of self-care to which I had to adhere. My immune system had been depleted seven years earlier, with six months of PICC line antibiotics. Medical professionals don't help you to fix the problems that antibiotics cause. They don't even mention that there could be an issue. It's up to us to make sure that we are researching how to get our immune systems back after prolonged antibiotic use.

The first year after breast cancer was challenging. I worked diligently to ensure that my body was the best it could be. I began pushing myself in my wheelchair a couple of miles a day and eventually started feeling healthier. I held on to hope, and I was not letting go! I worked on my mind and spirit, as well. I journaled, and I have worked through a plethora of childhood issues since then. It may sound funny, but I think cancer may have saved my life. I was a product of my environment that had convinced me that I was someone I wasn't. I was finally able to see myself for who I am. I became acquainted with my true self. I like who I truly am. I didn't like who I had been convinced I was. She was awful, but I would play the role every time.

The past two years have brought some of the biggest life challenges. Poet Maya Angelou said that nobody makes it out here alone. She was right. We must have people who love us. Otherwise, life isn't worth living. I have learned that a family is a group of people who love you, not necessarily a blood relationship. I am grateful that I have love in my life from people who stand by my side no matter what. Isn't it funny how we find these people who were once perfect strangers, and they become family?

Hope is what keeps us going when it feels like we are at the bottom of the well. Love is what pulls us out of that well. And, ordinary oneness is what connects us to everything in our environment.

From a very young age, I understood that we are all connected to everything in our environment. I was four years old that warm summer day. It was back in the days when you would find your friends by looking up the street to the driveway where the bikes were parked. I went outside to see if I could spot the other kids' bikes. No one was around. I sat down in the grass, putting my crutches next to me. I sat for a while, under the tree, enjoying the sunshiny day. A few minutes later, a Jaybird landed in the grass. I started talking to him. He screeched and squawked.

I sat there for a while longer, and then I decided it was time to go inside. I looked at the Jaybird and said, "Come on, let's go." I got myself up onto my crutches, and then I walked through the open garage to the door into the house. The bird was following right behind me. I opened the door into the house from the garage; let's hopped the Jay. Walking past my mom's sewing room, she was busy sewing dresses for my baby sister and me. I said, "Mom, I'm going to play with this bird in my room." She answered with a calm "ok." The Jaybird followed me into my bedroom. He hopped around my room, appearing to be checking things out. Then it got wild when he began to fly circles around my bedroom near the ceiling, squawking like mad. I was laughing because I thought the bird was playing with me. My mom came down the hall, threw open my door, and started screaming, "What is that bird doing in here?" I said, "Mom, I told you I was going to play with this bird in my room." She thought I was playing make-believe. The neighbor came over and was able to remove the bird from the house safely. Since then, I have had so many animal experiences that seem out of the ordinary, like the time I hand fed a raccoon mother. I would sit by the sliding glass door with the window cracked about an inch while the raccoon and her puffball babies ate, gaining her trust. One day, I decided to hand her a slice of bread. I was sitting on the floor with the slider cracked enough to get my arm through. I held onto one part of the bread, making sure there was plenty of area for the raccoon to take it.

My first concrete understanding of ordinary oneness was my connection to animals. We have a link to everything and everyone: the people, animals, and nature. I have become the type of person who always talks to the animals, and I speak kindly to my plants, too. There has never been a time in my life when I needed or wanted support or love that the universe didn't provide. If you align with the universe, it takes care of you with the people and situations it brings to you, even the challenging ones. It brings me comfort to know we are all connected.

Bio

Amy I. King is a Certified Life Coach/owner of Your Phenomenal Life, LLC. She taught in public education for a decade. She is a contributing author of international bestsellers: Inspirations: 101 Uplifting Stories for Daily Happiness, Manifestations: True Stories of Bringing the Imagined into Reality, The Grateful Soul: The Art and Practice of Gratitude, and The Courageous Heart: Finding Strength in Difficult Times. When not writing, she enjoys music, movies, art, travel and time with loved ones. Amy has overcome a plethora of challenges from which she draws wisdom to assist clients. Amy's greatest joy is using her personal experiences and to help others move past their personal blocks and outdated beliefs to becoming empowered to live the life of their dreams. Every challenge, she believes, is put before us to help us to evolve and grow into the greatest version of ourselves. Her relationships with clients are built on trust and vulnerability. She is currently coaching and writing her first solo book, Messy Wheels: Stories from Where I Sit, available on Amazon in 2021. She welcomes the opportunity to work with you to help transform your life!

yourphenomenallife585@gmail.com

or (916) 718-0914 text/call.

One with Trees
By Becki Koon

*Close your eyes and imagine sitting in a beautiful forest
filled with vibrant trees. Your back is supported by the
fragrant warm wood of a majestic tree that rises above you,
reaching up to the sky. You breathe in the fresh and clear
energy that surrounds you and exhale stress, resting into a
state of calm and peace, at one with the world. Ordinary or
extraordinary?*

I've had an affinity with trees for as long as I can remember; they naturally seem to call to me. I remember
being fascinated by all the different kinds of trees I
encountered. As a child, it was exhilarating to climb up, in
and amongst the gnarly branches of the old apple trees that
stood in a row in the backyard of my home. There was one
special tree in which the branches grew out of the trunk in
just the right way so I could step up into the center, with
large branches growing in each direction, strong and
inviting. I would boldly inch my way along the lower limbs
as far as I dared, exhilarated by my bravery. I remember the
smell of warm wood and the feel of rough bark under my
small hands. The aroma of apple blossoms in the spring,
followed by red and green apples in the fall, was intoxi-
cating to my young senses. I felt comfortable in the
branches of those old trees as if safely held, enveloped in a
gentle, calm energy, like the comfort of being home. It was
no wonder that, as I grew older, I wanted to maintain my

love and connection to the trees through creating beauty in the form of landscape design.

That love led me to a degree in Landscape Architecture. Funny how something that seemed like a passing childhood fancy could have such a significant impact on my future decisions and into the rest of my life. At the time, I believed I was drawn to Landscape Architecture out of my desire to be creative. The memories of childhood tree-sitting were just a background murmur. Of course, being creative was a factor but, as the years went by, I began to grasp the depth and breadth of my early connection and the deeper meaning I so instinctively understood at a tender young age.

When my ex-husband and I looked for a place in Montana to move, I was drawn to the Bitterroot Valley in the western part of the state due to the trees. The majestic Ponderosa pines were stunning. Many of them took my breath away while gazing at their beauty and presence. One tree, in particular, resonated deep within my soul. Every time I drove by it on the highway, my body felt chills, the hair on the back of my neck and arms stood straight up, and tears welled in my eyes. There was immense power in that connection, and yes, the trees played a major role in our decision to move to the Bitterroot Valley.

Later, in the late nineties, I experienced a vision quest in Idaho's wild, rugged mountains. On that journey into self-discovery, I felt much more than an intellectual connection to the large plants we call trees. I found myself in a state of *knowing* my relationship was so much more, realizing trees had always been communicating with me at some level, speaking to me through a means I could not explain, defying logic and intellect.

The week-long vision quest was facilitated by a seasoned outdoor adventure organization. They gathered people from different walks of life, living all across the United States. We camped together for seven days and participated in activities designed to set the stage for a three-day solo journey of self-awareness. The vision quest was life-changing for me, multi-faceted and deeply spiritual. Trees were one crucial aspect of that mystical journey; just how important I would soon discover.

Throughout the quest week, I was drawn to trees at every turn. During the four days of preparation, I noticed and became aware of trees from a heightened state of perception. More than once, I found myself sitting on large fallen pines or in branches, feeling the familiar comfort from childhood. Magic filled the air as I watched an almost hidden trickle of water wind its way through the moss-covered roots of a tall pine, closing my eyes so I could hear the subtle symphony being performed. I leaned my back against the bark of a majestic old-growth pine while in meditation, letting its warmth envelop me. I was mesmerized into no-time by watching ants crawl all over a large broken-down stump, offering the industrious insects some crumbs from a cracker. I performed a personal ceremony in an amazing natural tree circle that felt sacred and ancient. I witnessed the process of life through a new and vibrant sapling growing up and out of a decaying log, the old log providing sustenance for the spirited young tree. I found fabulous rocks of all shapes and sizes hidden in tangled root systems of toppled-over trees. The symbology of trees continued to show up everywhere I looked, and I felt the message was unmistakable; I knew I had to take notice. The question was, would I listen to the silent yet strong whispering voice of the trees?

While I was camping on my three-day solo, I pitched my tent where it was cradled within the exposed root systems of several trees in a small grove. A small underground stream, hidden by the trees, surfaced just a few feet from my tent door, flowing over moss-covered roots and rocks into a beautiful overland trickle of sparkling mountain spring water. Amidst the trees and roots, I felt protected and safe, as if these sentinels of the earth were my family. I was becoming conscious of their song, the messages they were imparting, and I listened.

One day during my solo quest, I found an area next to a mountain trail that had experienced a microburst, a place where strong winds had blown down and uprooted many trees, all at once, laying the trees on the ground in the same direction. I stood in awe of nature and marveled at the beauty of exposed root systems, intricate and naked as they were. Roots are the silent and unseen foundational support for the beautiful form we see as the green splendor above ground. The root systems perform their function without recognition, without boast, the silent director behind the scenes. That unseen dimension of the tree is critical to its survival. Without roots, the tree could not perform its life-giving transpiration function that supports the life force we experience on the planet's surface. I felt like the roots, with much of who I was hidden in the depths of my soul.

Many spiritual leaders have said trees are a multi-dimensional life force. While they cannot move, each tree resides in its own sacred spot, a place of energy trans-ference on many levels. The root system is in the second dimensional plane of Earth, drawing energy for its life force from deep within the core of the planet, pulling strength and nourishment into its upper realms. The third-dimensional plane is what we see on the planet's surface as the trunk that carries life-giving sustenance and water to its upper reaches to grow strong enough to perform its mission. The branches and leaves reach into the fourth-dimension of the sky, utilizing nourishment from the earth to co-mingle with the sun's energy, transforming the very air we breathe. The tree reaches into higher dimensions of existence, at which point it shoots this life-giving energy back through its structure into Earth, thus completing a cycle divine in nature, a circle-of-life for the benefit of all the planet's air-breathing creatures.

I realized trees hold healing properties beyond scientific explanation, beyond the tangible to the unseen mysteries of energy and vibration. Trees are healers of human energy, healers of our toxic emotional and energetic bodies. How often have you rested against a tree, felt the warmth of the bark, and, without knowing why, felt a calmness begin to caress your soul? That is because trees transform energy, transmute it, and dissipate it into Earth, a cleansing that goes way beyond oxygen for breath. They help humanity without humanity's awareness of them doing so. They do this silently and with a deep love for assisting. This is one reason people are so drawn to nature, a park, their yards, places where they can escape the busyness of life by finding a forest or a grove. The healing that takes place when they do is palpable, even if they are unaware. Trees are an integral part of that healing experience. The beauty of this process is humans do not have to recognize what is taking place for it to occur. It happens in the unseen realm, much like the root structures beneath the surface of visual awareness. All we have to do is breathe in and take in the gift of the trees, breathe out and release energy for transmutation.

It has been many years since my vision quest high in the mountains of Idaho, but the power of the trees and the messages they imparted have remained in my soul. I have continued to listen; I experienced an awakening during that time. Perhaps it would be more appropriate to say a remembering, a remembering of my deep childhood connection.

While walking down the road near my house, I was guided to gaze up into the higher reaches of the pines growing along the river. I looked into those beautiful branches full of dark green needles with the backdrop of a baby-blue sky and was moved to tears. I felt the familiar tingle of energy move up and down my spine as I gave reverent thanks to the trees for the silent support they provide to all of life.

It was then my gaze focused on one of the many beetle-killed trees inhabiting this forested area of Montana. I found myself giving thanks to those reddened trees for life and then for the sacrifice they made to benefit humanity. It was as if the intense whisper of the trees moved through me, and I was given an understanding of the depth of what that really meant. If trees do, in fact, heal and help humans transform their toxic energy bodies by transmuting that energy and dissipating it, then it made complete sense these trees were performing the ultimate sacrifice of love by dissipating the extreme levels of human toxicity residing in the world today. The beetles are just an outward manifestation of the weakness they experience; the overload of toxicity could no longer be transmuted and sustain life. I honored that awareness and thanked them for their selfless act. They now have the opportunity to provide both sustenance for new young plant life to grow and fuel for humans to heat their homes during cold winter months.

We could all learn from trees by understanding the subtle energies we experience and our relationship to supporting and living life multi-dimensionally, by understanding our connection to all things through unconditional love and acceptance. It is most important to listen for the still, silently whispering voice that carries power beyond our comprehension. Are you willing to listen and hear what the voice has to say? What if it comes from a tree?

The trees continue to whisper, to support our life force, and to impart the wisdom of the ages. I believe it is time to honor, respect, and become attuned to our energetic ties to these sentinels of Earth. It is our conscious evolution, compassionate awareness in action. It is this awareness our friends, The Trees, and our Earth Mother, Gaia, patiently await. Are you ready to step into oneness?

Bio

Becki Koon is a Heart-based Energy Intuitive/Spirit Medium, Reiki Master, HeartMath Coach, Life Coach,

Crystal Practitioner, and Author/Speaker. Through her business, Step Stone, Becki empowers people to seek their inner wisdom while holding space for them to heal, discover, and grow into the next highest version of themselves. She likes to refer to herself as the mid-wife of birthing a person's remembrance of their divine essence or purpose.

While Becki's background is broad, all of her experiences have a common thread—her passion for helping people, the land, animals, and the community through heart-centered compassionate action. Becki believes in the inter-connectedness of all things. She says, "I have come to embrace there are three aspects to the person I am: 1) coming from heart-centered action, 2) communicating with integrity, and 3) having vision to see the incredible potential in all beings on and off the planet. I am excited to be part of bringing Spiritual Ecology, Unity Consciousness, and Spirit Connection to the forefront of conscious awareness in the mass population."

stepstone2you@gmail.com
www.beckikoon.com
www.facebook.com/becki.koon.consulting
amazon.com/author/beckikoon

The Creation and
Dissolution of Karma
By James Masters

There is a lot of talk about karma in the world, but in my observations, there are few people who understand the concept. Most people's conceptualizations of karma are that it is a punitive system that punishes people for doing wrong. In fact, it is often a statement of vengeance that the afflicted will make when they are hurt. "Karma will get them."

Everything we experience is an effect of a cause. Karma is not a one-sided form of justice to punish our oppressors. If we the betrayed decry the betrayer, we are abdicating our own responsibility for the situation.

Karma is not a means for vengeance; it is a principle or a law. It is one of many metaphysical laws that we engage with in our physical time and space reality. Such principles and laws are meant to help *all* of us evolve.

Karma is a law that has its roots in the Law of Mind in Action and the Law of Attraction. These interconnected laws facilitate all our manifestations. These two laws are often referred to in metaphysical circles to teach people how to *manifest* new experiences. However, before we can manifest the new, we must first recognize that everything we have ever experienced is a manifestation.

"What does this have to do with karma?" you may ask. Well, karma means that whatever behaviors you have practiced, whatever you have *given out*, will come back to you. It is as simple as that. There are several principles within these two primary laws. Some of them are considered "higher laws" and others "lower laws." Like the different and sometimes seemingly contradictory laws within the Laws of Physics.

One of the Laws of Physics is the Law of Gravity, which for much of history kept humans in a dream state regarding our ability to fly. Our ancestors were seemingly bound by this lower law. However, as the Laws of Aerodynamics were discovered and understood, we began to utilize them to lift us off the ground. The higher law does not break the lower law, but it does transcend it.

This must be understood if we are to break free from the restrictions of karma and transcend into intentional creative potential. This is why it is important to understand how the laws work and why certain laws allow us to transcend the *lower* laws.

The first law is the *Law of Mind in Action*. In early metaphysics, there was a lot of talk about how the universe itself was mind and creative potential. It has been said that we are a "thought in the mind of God." It is also said that we are created in the image and likeness of God, which means we have the potential to use our minds to create our own experiences.

Another way of explaining the Law of Mind in Action is this way. What we choose to believe about ourselves and about life becomes true for us. Our thoughts become things. Some may say, "I have thought about becoming a million-aire for years, and I still do not have it." This may be true, but often when people are attempting to exert their mental power toward a goal, they are doing so without a full understanding of their motivation. Some want to manifest millions because they feel unstable or insecure. So, what is the thought being held in mind? The affirmation may be, "I am a millionaire," but the motivation is, "I am unstable and insecure." So, they receive based on this core intention.

The second primary law is more well known these days. It is the *Law of Attraction*. The Law of Attraction simply means that like attracts like. It is the reason why the affirmation for our proverbial potential millionaire does not work. Their words might be wealth, but their "point of attraction" is instability and insecurity. They may even be successful in attracting the money that they say they want, but without aligning with the quality that they desire, the stability and security, the money will do nothing for their experience of life.

The Law of Karma is a law that is subject to these two primary laws. Karma is intrinsically connected to these two laws, just as the two primary laws are connected to each other, and it all always starts in the mind. Everything that we experience is the "mind in action."

So, how does karma work? Karma starts with the undesirable thought often, fear or worry. Let us use the example of betrayal. Let us say in a past life you wanted to manifest a million dollars, but at the core, you felt very unstable and insecure. Sound familiar? You recognized an opportunity that could make you wealthy, but the only way you could achieve this goal is to go behind a friend's back. Your focus was so intent on the money that you decided to do it, and you betray your friend. This sets a pattern in your subconscious mind, what is often referred to as a "karmic debt."

Most of us have incarnated on this planet multiple times and have several of these karmic debts. Now we have incarnated into this life, and things are going great until we meet someone that is a perfect match for our karmic debt. We meet someone who will reflect to us our old pattern. They betray us, so what do we do? We say to ourselves and others, "Karma will get them someday!"

Now we are back to the beginning. This is what we must recognize if we are to ever be free from these karmic ties. You see, our experiences of karma are never related to another person's behavior. When someone betrays us, the karma we experience is the resentment, blame, and desire for vengeance that we hold in our minds about the other person. Karma is not something that will "get them." It is the energetic pattern we hold for ourselves.

The good news is that there is a higher law. Just like the Laws of Aerodynamics allow us to fly, there are higher laws that can pull us out of our old patterns. For as long as we hold on to things like fear, worry, resentment, blame, guilt, desires for vengeance, criticisms, and judgments, we will create those experiences. The Law of Mind in Action will constantly make it so.

Therefore, many people experience the same challenges repeatedly. They may be affirming or declaring the opposite, but their words do not match their motivation. This is the wisdom of the Law of Karma. Its purpose is not punishment but breaking free from these cycles and patterns.

The laws that free us from the density of karmic energy are the Laws of Forgiveness. These laws help us achieve flight in our lives, and in doing so, we can reach our desired destinations. In more than one esoteric tradition, it is said that "All forgiveness is self-forgiveness." In many ways, this is true. We do have to direct our forgiveness at others, but as we do, the Law of Attraction reflects this forgiveness back to us.

When we forgive, we are essentially setting other people free from karma, and this freedom then becomes our own point of attraction. Instead of being bound by past behaveioral patterns, we are given the freedom to choose a new pattern, and our intentional manifestations become more effective.

The Laws of Forgiveness are comprised of three laws. The Law of Love, the Law of Joy, and the Law of Peace. These laws facilitate the evolution of our own consciousness, which in turn allows us to become the masters of our own lives rather than the victims. When our core motivations are love, joy, and peace, then that becomes our point of attraction, and we create more love, more joy, and more peace in our lives.

Forgiveness is love because there is only one love. I have heard people talk about "unconditional love," but I do not believe in such a thing. This comes from a confusion between love and emotional attachment. Emotional attachments, especially romantic ones, can often be based in a lot of fantasy. Attaching emotions to mental images is not the

188

same thing as love because we are attaching our emotions to a false image. Our conjured ideas about another person are not the person.

This kind of emotional attachment creates a sense of painful longing, and the challenge with this is that painful longing becomes the point of attraction, and pain can only attract more pain. Love is different. Love always begins with the self and expresses outward. As Louise Hay used to say, "The door to the heart opens inward."

Love is our ability to accept and approve of ourselves as we are. Love is our own ability to see ourselves as perfect, just as we are. We are already perfect. We have manifested all our experiences perfectly, and we are already the perfect out-picturing of our current state of consciousness. Yes, we will evolve, grow, and change, but recognizing our perfection in the moment unlocks our ability to change in positive ways.

When speaking of forgiveness, we must forgive ourselves first by taking responsibility for everything we have created for ourselves. Recognizing all our experiences in life as a manifestation of our own state of consciousness. Yes, many of us have manifested through fear, but we have also manifested love, and the more we align with this one love, we will manifest more love with ease.

As we acknowledge the truth about ourselves, it becomes easier to recognize the truth about others. Every person on the planet is doing the best that they can based on the level of consciousness that they are at now. If they hurt us, it means that they had been hurt, and the pain of fear we both held attracted us to each other. Love is our ability to accept ourselves and others without constantly trying to change them.

The Law of Joy is related to the expression of love. Love allows us to express ourselves more freely, and this freedom brings about joy. Joy is freedom from worry, fear, and the past. The past really has no power over any of us unless we give it power. The constant fear of repeating old patterns is one of the surest ways to recreate them. As we release these old patterns, we become free to be ourselves.

In many spiritual traditions, joy is equated with strength. Phrases like, "The joy of the Lord is my strength" are common. Joy is empowerment. It gives us the freedom to say yes to the right things and no to the things that diminish us. Too often, people are afraid that if they love others, they will become a doormat, but the truth is that when we love, we lose the inhibitions that keep us trapped in what people refer to as "toxic relationships." Our authentic expressions will not put up with nonsense in any form.

The final Law of Forgiveness is the Law of Peace. Peace comes through trusting the intelligence of the one love to bring us our highest good. Our capacity to be peaceful is our ability to trust. Many people have told me that they have difficulty trusting in relationships, but without trust, there really is no relationship. There is only the idea of the relationship.

Trust comes from understanding how the world works and how our minds work. It also recognizes that this life is a process, not an event. Our desires are fulfilled in an unfolding format, and each moment of our lives has value and meaning. The more we trust, the more we can see the blessings that exist in each moment of our lives.

The truth is that we are already free, but to experience this freedom, we must also release anything in our own minds that contradict it.

Bio

James Masters is a contributing author in *The Courageous Heart: Finding Strength in Difficult Times* and *The Grateful Soul: The Art & Practice of Gratitude*. James is a Master Emotional Freedom Technique practitioner and Master Thought Field Therapy practitioner. He also does intuitive and spiritual coaching based on the New Thought traditions. If you want more information about James' work, you can go to his website: www.jamesmasters.net.

The Blessings of Oneness
By Evelyn McCaffrey

As I contemplated the title of this book, *Ordinary Oneness*, and reflected on its meaning in my life, what I was struck with was that, for me, finding ordinary oneness was anything but simple. I am on a quest, very common for those of my (mildly advanced!) age, to choose very carefully where and how to spend my time, my thoughts, my efforts. Centering to find what matters most to me, slowing down to find and feel the simple essence of me is requiring more being, less doing, and it is humbling to discover that that is not easy for me.

As I anticipated my upcoming retirement, I realized that I had spent many years of my life juggling lots of balls in the air: raising three lively sons as a single mom, working full-time and then some as a special education teacher, more recently remarrying and becoming involved with my new stepfamily as well, including providing some caretaking for stepfamily members with some special needs.

It began to dawn on me, as I dashed from home to school and back again, that I needed to prepare myself for a life that was not as crazy-busy as the life I was leading, and I felt a wave of relief even contemplating that new reality. What would that feel like? And then...how can I bear to wait another year for that beautiful chapter to begin?!

As it happened, I saw a possibility ahead that I had only dreamed of for most of my life: to look for an affordable getaway in view of a lake or river. I had dreamed for years of writing in an upstairs picture window overlooking a view of water. Was it possible that we could make this a reality?

My husband Wally resisted the idea of buying a second home, and I realized that this was more than a dream for me. This was a need I felt in a deep place in my heart. I did not understand it completely, but I trusted my heart. I stood firm and told him, "I do not understand all the reasons why, but this is something I need. If I am not sufficiently your partner to have input into 10% of one of your three retirement accounts (for the down payment), I am ready to say goodbye and accomplish this on my own." And I meant it. It felt amazing to have the strength to honor this deep intuition, even though I did not fully understand why it was so important to me. But it was.

I am a giver, and I give with joy. But I needed to con-sciously give this to *myself* at this critical time. I had found out that if I taught for one more year, I would be adding hundreds of dollars monthly to my pension, among other things. I needed to do something meaningful with that money, in a heart and soul way, to make this challenging last year worthwhile in a spiritual sense, aside from the deep joy that I found in teaching my students with special needs for so many years.

Buying our getaway has been one of the best decisions of my life. I needed a place to step off the fast-moving (but rewarding!) treadmill that my life had become and to help transition to a slower pace, a simpler rhythm, in a more rural place. The quiet at night, the beauty of the sunrise, the reflection off of the lake, the deer and birds so close...these touched my heart and soul in irreplaceable ways.

Our getaway with a lake view was a great start, but I knew I needed help to shift my perspective from *doing* to *being*. One resource I thought of was the author and life coach Cheryl Richardson, whose blog had been coming weekly to my inbox for years. I loved what she had to say about making conscious choices to honor her spirit, to be present in the moment, to practice self-care, all steps to "living your best life," something she wrote and spoke about often. I registered for her "Self Care by the Sea" retreat for the October following my last year of teaching, and I felt the excitement and anticipation of that for months! What an amazing time of choice, of reflection, I was entering with my retirement! What a luxury to be able to stop working in my 60s when so many do not have that option. I felt very grateful and very fortunate...and I still do.

As it happened, I ended up postponing that wonderful retreat, overlooking the ocean in Maine, for an even rarer opportunity – to take my three sons to see our Chicago Cubs play in the World Series, 2016! What better use could there possibly be for my retirement bonus?! And what a magical week that was! My oldest son Kevin is a comedian in New York, but he loves the Cubs so much that he has hosted a podcast for years, so he came out for the whole week. My youngest son Pat, in medical school at the time, gave us his "Hamilton" matinee tickets he could not use, and Kevin and I enjoyed it immensely! My middle son Joe was busy teaching, but he was up for joining us as soon as school let out. My three grown sons managed to see all seven games together, and I loved that they got so much joy from that! I flew Kevin's wife out from New York to join us, and the wives and girlfriends watched many of the games with my sons, in pubs or in their living rooms. The World Series game itself was a memory we will cherish forever, with a great and merry group around us. The best part of that was sharing our love of our team, our love of the game, and our love for each other in one giddy mix! That experience of oneness in the moment felt *so* extraordinary! *And* the Cubs became World Champs – bonus!

As months went by, I savored the opportunity to go almost weekly to our getaway, usually with Wally, sometimes overnight on my own. Each time we drove there (only 90 minutes away), I could *feel* the tension leave my body. What an incredible gift to be able to slip away so often and just relax! My husband was a superstar at relaxing, at home or anywhere, but I was a real novice. Our children enjoyed the novelty and beauty of our place, about 100 yards up from the lake but a view of it from almost every room.

I realized that the gifts of this getaway were many and varied. As I mentioned, perhaps because it was bought with that purpose in mind, I was able to truly relax here better than anywhere else on Earth. I found and took the time to marvel at sunrises over the lake, in all their changing moods and breathtaking colors. I was filled with awe and delight as deer wandered across our yard and up our driveway (when we were lucky!). I enjoyed sharing this experience with our children, and we bought a very used pontoon boat to motor around the lake as well. I found that there was a place where I could simply *be* and that that helped me discover layers of myself I did not remember.

My parents and grandparents brought us to that lake as we were growing up, for the day, or a weekend, or a week at a time, over the course of decades. So I felt close to my departed family here as well. I remembered times that I thought I had forgotten. So I always said prayers of thanks for the continuously unfolding gift of this special place. Its simplicity was one of its greatest gifts to me, but its gifts were too numerous to name.

Another passion in my retirement took me away from home and getaway; it helped me find greater oneness with those who were hurting and those who were helpers. When I heard about children being "detained" in child prisons and separated from their parents, my horror was too great to permit me to stay removed from this. I flew down to the border to protest, on my own the first time, but my late connecting flight meant I missed the protest altogether. I drove around Tornillo, Texas, in 102-degree heat, looking with sadness at the enormous tents that had hundreds of children in them, in freezing cold air-conditioning, with aluminum blankets and no parents. My heart nearly broke. All my life, I had devoted to making children's lives better, my own children's and my students' lives, and this was traumatizing children on purpose—appalling!

I connected online and by phone with refugee groups, having heard about the group "Grannies Respond," older women like me who wanted to help these children in any way they could. Over the next two years, some of the most meaningful experiences of my life occurred as I met and protested with amazing, fierce, passionate women and men from all over the country. We were "witnesses," as Joshua

Rubin came to call this heartfelt response, "witnesses at the border."

I spent two weeks in June 2019, with many witness friends in Homestead, Florida, where another detention camp for children had been established, after the Tornillo camp was closed with pressure from witnesses, among others. The heat was fierce, but the feeling of a shared mission that drew us together was even more intense. We felt a deep bond as we climbed up on ladders and called to the children, as they were marched around the exercise yard in high heat, "Besos y abrazos!" "Kisses and hugs!" as we waved big red hearts above our heads. We wanted them to know someone cared, someone saw them, someone sent love to them. They would take off their baseball hats and wave them and make whooping sounds, so dear...and we would climb down when they went inside and cry for them. Such an emotional experience created a major bond among us, teachers and grandmas from Alaska and New York, Chicago and San Antonio, Florida and Seattle. We felt at one with the children, at one with each other.

Two weeks after I returned to suburban Chicago, I replied to a social media post asking if anyone had any experiences to share about detention for an upcoming protest. I was asked to speak to a few thousand people in Daley Plaza, and, although the topic was tough, I felt compelled to share what we experienced in hopes of mobilizing more efforts and protests on behalf of the children. I felt grateful to have something to offer and to again be a witness to terrible actions being taken in our name.

Last winter, I was able to join our group of witnesses at Brownsville on the Texas border this time. Once again, the sense of oneness, of being united for the wellbeing of children and their families, was a strong bond between us. This time, we were even able to help the very few families that were allowed to cross that week, with the urging of the congressional delegation and heightened attention from the press. I am so grateful to have the freedom to join my friends, my fellow activists, for actions that I believe in so passionately.

So, as I reflect again on the topic of ordinary oneness, my perception is that the simplicity of everyday love, grace, and hope are anything but simple and anything but ordinary. When we choose our actions, our direction, our lives to reflect the deepest parts of ourselves, these become extraordinary reflections of our authentic selves. When we find great people and inspiring places that are in harmony with those truest parts of ourselves, that brings us joy, and delight, and a deep sense of oneness and belonging, one of life's greatest rewards.

Bio

Evelyn McCaffrey has loved to write her whole life, starting with her diary as a girl and continuing with journaling for her whole adult life. Her husband Wally is her mentor in the serious business of learning to relax in retirement! Her sons Kevin, Joe, and Pat are all grown up now, but they led her on a merry dance in her 15 years as a single teacher mom, and she loved the chaos, the laughter, and the help from her "nanny," their beloved Sheltie,

Shannon. Their wonderful wives (Jaimie, Natalia, Julie) have become dear friends, and Joe and Natalia had a baby girl this year who is her Nana's pride and joy! Ev met her stepdaughters Jenny and Erika as full-grown adults and enjoys being part of their family, too, with Erika's husband John and their two great sons. Ev's passions are hanging with family; attending Kevin's comedy shows; snuggling her dogs; helping children; writing; activism on behalf of children; appreciating nature; singing and playing show tunes on the piano; staying in touch with friends on social media; scrapbooking; traveling; all time spent with grandchildren, watching them in sports or playing on the floor—and relaxing with reading!

The Magical Affirmation Effect
By Paula Meyer

I was thinking about affirmations the other day, and why they don't always work. I have certainly been guilty of going through my daily affirmations without really caring about them. I realized that most of the time, I give it a half-assed effort. Here is the definition of half-assed: done with little effort or care; incompetent or inadequate. Wow, that kind of stung!

It was also a revelation. If I think about the times where I have been incompetent or inadequate, it was because I didn't really care about the task at hand. I didn't put the energy into it, to be deemed competent or adequate. I just didn't care enough to be successful.

I decided to add some humor to the subject about my affirmation challenges. I coined a new term for this: Half-affed, which means that affirmations are done in a rote way, with little effort or care.

So when I catch myself doing this, I lovingly say: It's not affin' working! I'm half-affin' it! Stop half-affin' it!

I've titled this the magical affirmation effect because effect is a consequence or outcome brought about by a cause. When we half-aff it, we bring about an effect that's an unintentional result of our non-action. When we give it a full-aff effort, we create the desired outcome we want because we took action.

Remember when you were a kid and said your nightly prayers,

Now I lay me down to sleep

I pray the Lord my soul to keep

If I should die before I wake

I pray the Lord my soul to take.

If we really felt that with feeling, we would be traumatized for life! We'd all be insomniacs! We've been taught to pray without really taking it to heart.

Or we pray or meditate from a victim mindset, and we really feel into that. And guess what? We keep finding more reasons to be a victim! And why is that? It's because we were feeling into being a victim while we were asking for help.

The same thing happens with our affirmations. We say them over and over without really feeling what it would feel like to be a reality. Then we get frustrated when they don't become our reality. When we repeat them over and over without any real feeling or care, we are reciting these by rote, and it becomes an unconscious exercise. It's like your affirmations are a radio station playing in the background. You can hear them, but you are not fully experiencing them.

Our minds can repeat things over and over while also thinking about something else. Our brain is accustomed to linear and logical learning, which makes it feel in control. When it feels in control, it becomes comfortable and then tunes out! When our affirmations are done in this fashion, the brain excels at the repetition and when we don't push our body to "feel into it." The brain relaxes and quickly tunes out. Can you see why this might be happening with your affirmation practice?

Every morning for over twenty years, I have been saying these three affirmations, three times each:

1. This day, I am my holy, holy divine spirit.
2. Bless this body and burnish bright my holy temple.
3. Let me execute my duties this day, from the just place of my Holy Spirit.

Most mornings, I have to start over at least three or four times! By the time I get to the third attempt, I finally begin to focus on the words and what they mean to me. I still love these affirmations, and they are what I want to be every day. My mind has just gotten used to saying them and glosses over the significance of them to get to the end, just like we might do with our tasks during the day. We rush to get to the end, so we can check it off our list!

Feelings are the key ingredient! The affirmation is the intention, and the feeling is the action. The action is critical! The main reason that we don't feel into it is because it's an unknown and we don't know what it feels like. But you can use a surrogate feeling after you state your affirmation! You can trick the brain and body into action, by remembering a feeling of exhilaration from a past event, say learning to drive a car, winning a game, going trick or treating, Christmas morning, or any event that made you feel enchanted or victorious. You can even take it a step further and act out that affirmation in your daily life so that you can then attach real-time feelings to it.

There are many amazing tarot card decks that we can use to help us with our intentional affirmations. Don't get scared by the word "tarot." The word itself can bring up feelings of fear based on misguided notions about the use of tarot cards. Our mind conjures up an image of a mysterious fortune teller dealing in black magic, who turns over the grim reaper card. Immediately we are fearful for our lives! Tarot cards are just another way to help us find our divine purpose, to tune into spirit for answers and guidance. And by tuning in, we develop the muscle memory of trusting our intuition.

You can find card decks designed around many subjects: angels, goddesses, animals, flowers, and simple words or statements of inspiration. The image on the card is essential in assisting you in creating the feeling that will resonate and inspire you to embody it. Remember, the body is critical in the process. It must really feel on a deep level and be entrained into the new reality you are attempting to create. It takes consistency and practice, just like learning to read and write.

A great way to work with card decks is to add Mother Nature to the process. Choose a card and go out in nature. Stand next to a tree, on the bank of a river or lake, or your favorite place in nature. Tune into the energy of the beauty around you. When you are feeling the beauty in your body, then put your focus on the card. Speak to your body as if it's your best friend (which it is!), and describe how it feels and how it will serve your purpose. The body listens to us, and it follows instructions. Your job, if you want to effect change, is to give it the best instructions you can!

Repetition is another important key. The body and mind need consistency to seat it into the subconscious. It takes a lot of practice and concentration to learn how to drive a car. You must learn the rules of the road, the feel of the car in your control, and your senses need to be in hyper mode to master the process. Over time and practice, it becomes unconscious. You know how to turn the car on, set the mirrors, use your lights and blinkers. It flows now, and you are more at ease. Then you can enjoy the freedom of driving while being aware of the scenery as you pass by. You can easily have a conversation with your passenger or sing along with the radio because you and your body are now at ease. What was once new and scary is now fun and adventurous. Take that same way of mastering anything into how you use card decks and affirmations.

You can even create your own card deck. It can be as simple as choosing 3-5 words that inspire you and resonate with what you want to be. For each word, draw a picture of what that word means to you. You don't have to be a talented artist to do this. Just feel into the word and draw what comes to mind. That image will become your talisman for that word, and each time you envision it, you can feel it. If your word is abundance, then draw what abundance means to you. It could be a simple beach scene, with the sea signifying all the abundance that is always available. Or it could be your dream house or car. It doesn't matter what the image is, only that it instills in you a sense of what it would be like to have that image as a reality.

You can also create your own Affirmation or Inspiration Jar. You can find these already set up online, so you just print them out and put them in your jar. Or you can create a simple word document with all the words you want to have in your jar. Pick one word daily or weekly and embody that word fully all day.

There are also other decks that provide ideas on things to do. One of my favorites is from Sunny Dawn Johnston, called "Fill Me Up." It's a self-care card deck, and you choose an activity to complete that increases your energy and self-love. It includes fun things like coloring, making a meal, sending love to others, connecting with water, singing a song, or decluttering—just easy and simple things that nurture us.

Affirmations are a great practice to put into place. Give yourself the gift of being a powerful effecter of your life.

Don't half-aff it! Give it a full-aff effort!

And then watch the Universe shower you with success!

Bio

Paula Meyer's mission is to help grieving women suffering from life-changing losses and tragedies. After becoming a widow at 54, she left her job and began a year of travel to find joy and purpose again. As her travel ended, the Covid-19 pandemic began. She used the same strategies of navigating the grief of her husband's death, for the grief from the pandemic and social unrest. She was confronted with losing her freedom, losing her normal life, and being thrown into the unknown as she was starting her business, and waking up every day to the same reality. Paula has more than 30 years of experience as an event planner and procurement/contracting specialist, with 12 years in author/speaker management. She has organized and managed 135 workshops around the world. As an avid traveler, she has visited 20 countries and 40 US states. Her company, GP Eventworx, specializes in event production for speaker/teacher workshops, as well as grief retreats for women. She is currently creating an Online Grief Summit and writing a book about her year of travel, debuting in early 2021, along with an online course based on the book. For more information, visit her website at www.gpeventworx.com.

Are The Little Things
Truly The Big Things?
By Maggie Morris

As I sit in the stillness of the morning sipping the nectar of the coffee gods, I ponder this question, "Are all the little treasured moments in life really the *big* moments of life?"

As you sit for a moment in your own serene space, seek your own answer to this question.

Oh, I know we all have those big moments such as the birth of a child, the excitement in a child's eyes on Christmas morning, graduation day, wedding day, landing that dream job, a first date with the hottie you have been dreaming of, finally getting that fantasy car, or that vacation of a lifetime, just to name a few. We may all have had many of those big moments in life that I refer to as "Cinderella moments," yet I believe it is truly the small ordinary moments that can be the most impactful in our lives. Those random moments have the ability to inspire greatness.

Using the Cinderella story as an example, it was not that fabulous night out with the handsome prince that made her who she was. She gained her beauty in the everyday toils of her life in her simple moments of working while singing, talking and dreaming with the mice and birds. Her beauty grew in the everyday kindness she gave to the unkind people in her life. That kindness she extended to her stepmother and those horrible stepsisters. Oh yes, that great ball was an extravagant party with wonderful moments, including the meeting of that handsome prince with all the happily ever after, but remember that was just one night, one ball, one party. The moral of my story is that Cinderella would never have gotten to that night, at the ball, had she not already found her joy in the everyday moments of her life. She found her joy in life long before the ball. She found her happily ever after before she ever met her prince.

Those simplistic moments in life that we often take for granted are, to me, the big things in life. The gratitude of that homeless person when you hand him a gift card for the local coffee shop. The smile on the senior's face when you randomly buy her some flowers at the grocery store. Holding the door for that mom struggling with her baby stroller. Offering kindness while waiting in a long line. Giving up your seat on the bus. Calling a friend just to let them know you're thinking of them. Extending a hand of kindness in a world that is often too busy to notice. Those are the ordinary greatness moments of life.

I extend to you this challenge: start to notice the little *big* moments of life. You will very quickly see the shift in your soul as your focus changes. You may find that your life is already full of many little miracle moments that may have previously gone unnoticed.

Other people may see a shift in your personal perspective as you begin to live life with eyes wide open to the limitless possibilities before you. You will not only believe in random miracle moments, but you will actively pursue them. Like me, you may anxiously await that cardinal coming to your kitchen window each morning to say hello. Like me, you may even live a life full of gratitude for every unexpected miracle moment.

Let me share an example of everyday love that happened to me a few weeks ago.

On one ordinary evening, after an ordinary day, in an ordinary week, I took my puppy, Connor, for our usual evening stroll through our neighborhood. I say evening stroll but what I really mean is that nightly bathroom walkabout while avoiding skunks, coyotes and other wild creatures that could wreak havoc on our otherwise uneventful evening walk.

Being early December, I took notice that one of the houses on our block had beautiful green lights brightly shining on both sides of the garage door. Upon arriving home, I casually mentioned to my partner that this house down the street has beautiful green lights on their garage. His response: "Really," with no other comment. A short time later, I see him putting on his jacket, so I inquire where he is going. His gruff response: "Just going to the hardware store." Yep, you guessed it, he went to our local hardware store to pick up some green lights. Simple random everyday love! Simple random kindness! I noticed! His love was shining brightly in that moment, much brighter than the green lights lovingly installed over our garage door.

Think back for a moment to the last time you gave or received an act of everyday kindness. Did it not spark something inside of you to respond with kindness or gratitude? Those random simplistic actions recharge and inspire us. Simple acts of kindness are infectious. Most human beings respond in a positive way to kindness. Try it out! Practice some simple random acts of kindness and see how people respond. See how you respond. How does your body feel? How does your soul feel? I often say, "Love is our superpower!" Engage your superpower!

We do not even realize the power we hold through love, hope and kindness. When we offer love, hope and kindness, we are a lifeline to a world drowning in hopelessness and despair. People in our world are often more concerned about status and careers than they are about integrity and being true to their authentic selves. People in our world are addicted and committing suicide at alarming rates because they have lost hope. Doctors prescribe medication and work at removing the symptoms of hopelessness but never get to the root of helping people overcome hopelessness. Our education system teaches various skills but often lacks teaching the skills needed to manage life.

I invite you to discover who *you* are and *be* that person instead of being who others say you should be. When we discover our true identity, we begin to stop searching for the big things in life. When we begin to step into that true identity, we can shed the ego-self and just *be*. When we step into that true identity, we can offer hope, love and kindness to those in our world who have lost the ability to hope or dream.

Many years ago, my son shared a poem with me that had impacted his life, and in turn, it also impacted my life. That conversation with my son gave me a different perspective on what was important in life.

Ordinary Oneness

That poem is named "The Man in the Mirror" but could have just as easily been named "The Woman in the Mirror."

"The Man in the Mirror"

When you get all you want, and you struggle for pelf,

And the world makes you king for a day,

Then go to the mirror and look at yourself

And see what that man has to say.

For it isn't your mother, your father or wife

Whose judgment upon you must pass,

But the man, whose verdict counts the most in your life

Is the one staring back from the glass.

He's the fellow to please,

Never mind all the rest.

For he's with you, right to the end,

And you've passed your most difficult test

If the man in the glass is your friend.

You may be like Jack Horner and "chisel" a plum,

And think you're a wonderful guy,

But the man in the glass says you're only a bum

Ordinary Oneness

If you can't look him straight in the eye.

You can fool the whole world,

Down the highway of years,

And take pats on the back as you pass.

But your final reward will be heartache and tears

If you've cheated the man in the glass.

Poem by Dale Wimbrow 1934

This poem reminds me that being authentic to ourselves is the goal in life. The rest is just stuff that matters not in the end.

Don't allow your search for those big things in life to steal away your joy in the everyday miracles that this life offers you.

In my own quest to discover my authentic self some years ago, I stumbled across or shall I say the universe put me into the path of a Mindfulness Coach and a great Australian modern-day guru, John Shearer. Through his teachings and the guidance of my own Soul, I discovered the little things truly are the *big* things in this life. I discovered that if I'm true to "The Woman in my Mirror," I truly have discovered happiness and fulfillment. I no longer needed to look for that pot of gold at the end of the rainbow because I am the gold, and my life is the rainbow offering light to others.

If you have lost your way and your light is dim, ask the creator of your inner soul to allow you to see the light of everyday love, hope and kindness in your world. Allow that light to guide you to your authentic self and begin your own journey to find that the little things truly are the big things in life. The life you save could be your own.

In my book *Journey to Soul* and John's book *Mindful Actions*, I believe you will find many everyday miracles offering hope in the ordinary oneness of our lives. I believe you will find that our ripple can help you discover your own ripple to light the world around you. We believe the power of love, light and mindfulness is a lifestyle of being in the present everyday moments of life.

I believe that we all have the power and ability to inspire others by the little things that we often think are insignificant: those moments of ordinary oneness in everyday life. Be that spark that fans the flame in others. That one small spark can ignite others to do the same, and the ripple grows into a huge river of change.

How you want this world to change begins with you. Be authentically you in the everyday and seek to be the best possible version of yourself. The creator of your soul is just waiting to assist you in that journey.

And like myself, you may find that the little things truly are the *biggest things*!

"In the Stillness"

By Maggie Morris

In the stillness

Of the morning

Ordinary Oneness

I hear my Spirit call

In the stillness
Of the morning
It echoes, can you hear me

I'm here
In the sun, on your face
In the air, that you breathe
I'm here
In the chirping, of the birds
In the ripple, of the stream
I'm here
In the stillness
Waiting for you

In the stillness
Of the morning
I hear my Spirit call
I'm here
Come sit with me
Let me trade
Your turmoil to Peace

Ordinary Oneness

Your fear to hope

Your anxiety to Calm

In the stillness

I'm here

In the stillness

Of the morning

I'm here

Come sit in Peace with me

I'm here

Come sit in my Love

In the stillness

Of the morning

Can you hear

Your Spirit call

Namaste

"I honor the place in you in which the entire universe dwells.

I honor the place in you which is of love, of truth, of light and of peace.

When you are in that place in you and I am in that place in me,

We are one."

215

Bio

Maggie is an authentic caring, sensitive soul with a passion for nurturing others with her soul love. Maggie lives her gifts of service to humanity through her generosity and her ability to ignite the flame in others to see their limitless possibilities. Maggie uses her intuition and connection with spirit to be an example of strength and courage to all she meets. As a Life Coach, Mindfulness Mentor, Meditation Facilitator, Death Doula, and Author, Maggie continues to pursue her passions as well as help those she connects with to find healing. You can reach Maggie through her website at www.whispersofwisdom.ca.

The Mirror That Reflects
My Core Beliefs
By Josefina Ochoa Meza

"What a catastrophe," screams every cell in my body. Facing an emotional breaking point, storming downhill on a roller coaster of emotions, gaining momentum by the millisecond, projected to hit the ground at full force as I witness my dear friend laying on the floor lifeless.

"Is this real? Am I living a nightmare?" reflects my body in shock.

November 19, 2014, a cold, chilly morning, and reality as I know it has officially collapsed! I lost everything I worked hard to achieve. At this point, what else will I manifest? A bird shitting on my head? Will I attract God himself descending from the heavens to kick me in the stomach as he laughs to my face?!

Betrayed is what I felt by the very Holy Spirit I placed my absolute faith in to guide me through the way.

"Why?" I whispered to my soul, disappointed and devastated because the law of attraction blew up in my face.

Intuition has always been my greatest gift. As a child, I somehow knew things, and not until I was older, I learned the labels to describe my abilities best; empath, clairsentient, and claircognizant.

Hearing God's voice inside of me, honoring Her wishes, was what I did best. This was my self-worth. So, what went wrong?

In 2007, I experienced my first perceived episode I refer to as "Dark Night of The Ego." I lost something I learned to love, someone dear to my heart, convinced God rewarded me for my good conduct. Losing what I perceived as "true love" is not something one's prepared to undergo. In fact, I was conditioned throughout my childhood to guard my heart against "trespassers."

I was sideswiped, forced to my knees, declaring I would never open my heart again. However, this declaration was short-lived. Destiny had a different ending written in the books.

Random people began approaching me, expressing how love is real and magical. "Still believe," they said.

Upon the third random approach, I knew God was speaking to me through them, advising me to trust the process. As an obedient student of God, I loosened the grip to resistance and began to attract the perfect literature to activate my DNA and jump-start my evolution. I realized this "love" I perceived lost was the very catalyst to inspire my journey inward, into an ocean of self-awareness.

I'm now 26, fighting for my mother's recovery; suddenly, everything goes dark, the world turns off. I am alone, isolated in a foreign country, trying to make sense of what I was hearing. On October 30, 2010, I faced my biggest nightmare; I lost my mother to a dirty old disease, cancer. My inner tsunami emerged, swallowing me into my second "Dark Night of The Ego."

My internal hard drive, identifying my whole existence, shattered. I lost the person I was most self-identified to.

"Who am I now without my mother? What's next?" I was forced to ask.

Deep-rooted "shadows" began to unravel before me. Undergoing major discomfort, I was compelled to rediscover myself. To unveil the truth behind Josie and reinvent the relationship dynamic I held between all aspects within me for the authentic version I longed to embody.

As I embraced my journey through the search for inspiration, unpacking who I am outside of my mother's perception of me, I tasted freedom, strengthening my faith in the concept many call, "law of attraction." Knowing, everything happens for a divine reason.

Through my self-discovery, I opened doors for deeper desires to be more love, wiser, and freer.

However, be careful what you wish for, for you might not like what you attract first into your reality to gain that which your soul truly desires.

In 2013. I became a vibrational match to the author, Barbara Marx Hubbard; her material inspired me to teach a self-empowering class called "The Wheel of Co-Creation." There, I became a byproduct of my teachings, further trusting my intuition to follow my "yeses" without second-guessing myself, welcoming synchronicities to manifest all around. As the signs got louder, more vivid my dreams became, and my out-of-body encounters began to feel more real than reality itself. I couldn't stop seeing the reflection of inspiration mirroring back to me from all angles. Everything occurring around me was a mere result based upon my revised choices and actions. Little did I know, I would be stepping into a new kind of reality, one that is governed by me, not by my authority figures nor childhood traumas. But first, it had to get worse before it got better.

As I continued to master attracting my deepest desires, leaping, and the net appearing, I intuitively was guided to move to Mexico. Just like that, with zero hesitance, I followed the call, moving to Michoacán, Mexico, in January of 2014. There, I launched a project to register a retirement home into a nonprofit organization, caretaking my sickly aunt, and orchestrated community service activities to spread awareness. Mexico was home for 1 year, 3 months. Proud of the life I was building, experiencing service to others and personal freedom, my greatest achievement thus far. However, 6 months into this experience, life lifted another veil, and everything shifted. My surroundings were no longer welcoming; resistance was the new melody echoing around town. Those of authority in this small town felt threatened by the light I carried; jealousy was the virus, preying on the weak. Although I noticed the shift, I held faith the Almighty had my back, for I had only been an obedient student, honoring the call, therefore impossible for the "light" to lose the battle against the "darkness," said the hope within. To my surprise, everything achieved in Mexico was disintegrating, one by one. Darkness declaring victory, as I witnessed the horrifying scene of Amador Garcia Ruiz, dead on the floor.

How could my intuition, synchronicities, vivid dreams, and out-of-body experiences intentionally lead me to failure? Wasn't I deserving? Did the universe conspire?

Defeated and depressed, I grasped to understand why I attracted these outcomes if I followed the manifestation equation to the T? How did I attract the opposite of what I wish to experience if I had tuned my vibrational frequency to faith and love? According to my knowledge, I should have manifested positive results?!

Determined to decipher the formula, I recalled Author Neil Donald Walsh's perception of resistance. If one is in the path of self-awareness, they are equally on the path to first attracting the very experiences one resists the most! Have you heard of the saying "what you resist persists?" Welcome to the story of my life.

So, what is resistance to manifestation?

Resistance is the attempt to avoid anything and everything making you feel uncomfortable, in any form whatsoever. It is merely the idea of pushing away or rejecting a feeling, emotion, or sensation within your felt perception that feels overwhelming.

Traumatic experiences are prime examples of circumstances you wish not to reencounter. It is the feelings in the body that remain unresolved that one wants to avoid at all costs. Unfortunately, with time, these unresolved traumas gain momentum the more you attempt to avoid them (resist); your emotions tend to highjack you without your consent, governing everyday life. You navigate life through the eyes of your inner wounded child while having zero awareness it's happening. With a distorted perception of life, the fractured inner child has been steering the wheel of your reality.

As living organisms, our nature is to balance itself. Our fundamental innate desire is to heal and integrate with the collective, to function as a sustainability unit. Therefore, divinely guided to Mexico to manifest a "beautiful, masterpiece of a mess," creating the perfect "tornado" to pull me back into the emotional state I feared the most for healing. Depression was too overwhelming, and I was never taught to address my emotions properly, so I fled. This unresolved emotional state of depression set the stage for my integration journey to evolve into a more sustainable human.

As I listened to my pain, using all senses, falling deeper into connection with the fragmented aspects dwelling within, I knew the time had come. I was finally ready to face my darkest inner demons and nurture them back into the woman I know myself to be. Reminded of a voice I heard in my dreams, "You are finally coming home."

Forced to stop running, turn, face the tornado, and step into the eye, was when I realized birthing a new kind of self-love. An unconventional love that accepts and embraces the very "darkness" I saw in the eyes of my father as a child. It was a kind of agony and despair I wanted to save him from, let alone admit I am equally a prisoner to it and had been for all these years.

As I fought myself internally, I courageously chose to parent my pain and begin a deeply intimate, vulnerable dialogue with my depression. It was the aspect of me I learned to reject, shame, and dissociate from since childhood. Depression was present in my felt perception, stronger than ever before, with a level of momentum to wipe out a city.

I vulnerably asked, "so, what happened? How did I become a match to everything I've lost?"

"I knocked many times, politely, and every single time I needed your attention, understanding, and validation, you rejected me, ignoring me as if I did not exist. Just because you wish not to feel me does not mean I do not exist inside of you. You cannot get rid of me nor destroy me. I Am energy. Energy can only be transformed, not destroyed or severed."

"Are you saying that by ignoring you, for the past 30 years, you've gained momentum with time, growing more powerful and destructive?"

"Precisely," said depression. "That what you resist inside of you persists to be balanced, healed as many of you describe. Resistance fuels the aspects in you that you wish to disassociate from. The more you attempt to push me away, the more you fuel me. What you're attempting to achieve is to get rid of you, sever yourself from the aspect that is equally you as well. Only through transmuting the energy into frequency more sustainable to the evolving human body can it shift and be integrated with the whole. Don't you yearn to feel whole, long for deep connection with others?"

"Yes, but I thought admitting to a "negative trait" would mean giving it life, calling it to fruition. I thought the more I focused on you, the more of you I would attract into my reality. So, I avoided you like the pledge."

"Did it work?" uttered depression.

"No!"

"That is the biggest misconception; only by admitting to the problem could you give me what I need. Feeding me the missing experience to the circumstances that got me in this traumatic state- will transmute my vibrational energy into a higher frequency, allowing integration to occur.

For example, an addict, when eventually choosing to admit to their problem, can then choose to rehabilitate, restoring themselves to health."

"Does that mean you, depression, yearn to be nurtured? Have you been seeking to be seen, heard, and understood, validated, and fundamentally accepted unconditionally in the exact emotional state you've been stuck in all these years? Hello?" (long pause) "Hello, are you still here?"

"I think; I don't know, I'm losing my identity, for I cannot sense myself as strong as I did before. Is this coming home?" in a faint voice, depression speaks.

And just like that, my depression, shame, and isolation began to feel understood. Collectively, working as a unit to gain the awareness that only through collaborating with all aspects, providing complete presence can we survive the internal war we all struggle with as humans.

When fully understood and practiced, the mirror will begin to reflect the inner peace within yourself in physical reality.

Bio

Josie is a Master Certified Emotional Healing Coach. Owner of Emotional Wisdom. She specializes in human emotions, mental distress, childhood trauma, somatic experiencing, breathwork, conscious fragmentation to integration work, and self-awareness. Josie was born extra-sensory. She identifies as an empath, clairsentient, and claircognizant. As a child, Josie suppressed and rejected her innate abilities due to the threat perceived they embodied. She lacked understanding, held limited awareness of its nature. Eventually, Josie unveiled these skill sets weren't a curse but rather an opportunity to transmute into the physical embodiment of "truth" and authentic self-acceptance. This transcendence didn't come easily. Josie faced deep depression, self-rejection, and shame, unconsciously imprisoned, a slave to these emotions. Her courageousness to embrace vulnerability was the golden ticket back home, into the truth. Josie integrated deep layers of fractured, distorted aspects of who she believed to be. Ultimately, experiencing the taste of inner peace, healing generational traumas. Josie's passion and purpose are to help end the internal wars we all battle within. True peace only begins to exist when you let go of resistance and practice the art of unconditional self-acceptance. Accept all of who you are right now, then observe your outer reality accept you back! For more information, visit Josie's website at Emotional-Wisdom.com.

Changing Trauma into Love, Grace and Hope
By Geneva Osawe, Ph.D., M.S.W., LCSW, LMFT, LCAC

Federal and State correctional institutions statistics tell us that African American males between the ages 18 and 65 are the largest group of the male population. This racial disparity, according to research, means that at least 25.1% of African American children will have a parent incarcerated by the time they are fourteen years of age. A large percentage of these children can be labeled as children coming from families living in perpetual crises, with these ongoing crises affecting normal family transitional periods. The families and children are plagued with many social ills, such as living in cities with food deserts, old and underfunded schools, homelessness and urban decay. Social stigma and social isolation have been experienced by the children within these families. These different institutional descriptions of incarceration may have reinforced the stigma and social isolation of these families.

These different traumatic experiences can lead to long-lasting and damaging effects on the child and the family. A fathers' incarceration can start a domino effect on the entire family system with the removal of the father from his parenting role. These traumatic events have led to these children became an invisible population with no voice.

Children with an incarcerated father of all ages developed behavior and mental health problems, experienced aggression, anger, foster placement, academic difficulties, including juvenile court involvement. In an effort to protect the children, family members can become dishonest and create untruth regarding fathers' absence and the reason for the absence, keeping secrets regarding the absence of the father.

The major problem for these children has been the manner in which their families and community have responded to these boys affected by the stigma of incarceration. Parents and extended family made the incarceration a secret.

Victor Frankl, in *Man's Search For Meaning*, explained in his writing that we cannot avoid suffering, but we can choose how to cope with it by having a renewed purpose with a message of hope.

When given an opportunity to have a voice, these children can develop programs such as Echoes of Incarceration, producing positive messages of hope and inspiration to other children who experienced the trauma of parental incarceration.

What would be different or changed if all the children in the world could develop similar programs modeled from Echoes of Incarceration and have mentors' support in developing projects that instilled a sense of healing, sharing and relationship building with the focus on restorative justice? These projects would bring out the secret into the open through inclusion and documentaries of hope, love and sharing. Michael would no longer see himself as remaining a pawn and never advancing to become a bishop or a rook. His life would be changed, and he would get off of the front row and began to speak love and hope into the lives of other children who have lived with the secret of losing a parent to incarceration.

What would happen if the secrets of the family were no longer a burden on the child? Children in these families could change the toxic, dangerous secrets into one of transformation, changing their negative experiences into forgiveness and love regarding understanding the trauma related to having an incarcerated parent. These changed perceptions of individuals and the community would cause a domino effect of seeing the incarcerated parent in the same loving way as their children view them. Showing everyday love could change negative relationships; resolve or mend broken relationships for the many families and children who have an incarcerated parent.

The world is comprised of all kinds of toxic secrets from individuals to institutions. However, the secret of incarceration can be a very dangerous and toxic secret affecting relationships and taking years to heal. The development of mercy and grace can lead to forgiveness and a resolution that changes these traumatic experiences into healing through individual projects. These children can tell their own stories, developing their own documentaries and becoming mini filmmakers, learning how to become journalists that supports hidden talents and the development of resilient traits. The last and most challenging is changing the prison system into one of a more social justice humane approach in understanding these children and their parents and developing positive programs to meet their needs.

Therefore, the solution to having an incarcerated parent is to provide the children and their parents and the family with supportive coordinated family services. Children with incarcerated parents have become so common, like ice cream and apple pie. However, they can become portraits of resilient youth who have been able to overcome the negative aspects of parental incarceration.

This public awareness campaign of these awesome children who have changed trauma into love and forgiveness could help reform the criminal justice system into one where all parents and their children could be seen in a positive fashion, changing this dragon and octopus nightmare for these children by reducing the stigmatizing label assigned to them. This outpouring of forgiveness by these children would change the well-being of all children who had or still has an incarcerated parent. This is a message of change, awareness, transformation, love and hope for all children with an incarcerated father.

Bio

Geneva Osawe (O-sou-wee) is a licensed clinical social worker, licensed marital and family therapist, and licensed clinical addiction counselor. She holds a doctorate of philosophy in Advanced Studies in Human Behavior from Capella University and an M.S.W from Indiana University, Indianapolis, Indiana. Additionally, she received specialized training in family studies from the Family Institute of Chicago/Center for Family Studies. She is the first professionally licensed social worker in the State of Indiana. She was a member of the professional licensing board for many years and participated in writing the requirements for licensing as a social worker and marital and family therapist. She is the founder-director of The Family Matters Institute, Inc., an outpatient family service organization. She provides clinical supervision for complex cases and state licensure. She specializes in providing culturally competent models for interventions to urban children and their families. Finally, she is a subject matter expert on children with incarcerated parents both academically and personally. Her son was incarcerated, and her grand-children suffered the same challenges that confronted her clients. Finally, she identifies herself as an urban behavioral sociologist that has worked with families affected by multiple social ills. Much of her thoughts and ideas on this subject are a result of her extensive dissertation research on children with incarcerated fathers.

Contact:
familymatters.inc@gmail.com
osaweg@hotmail.com

Morelli
By Kim Pence

Have you ever planned with heartfelt diligence the details for a special event like an anniversary, retirement party, or vacation, and then astonishingly, it all falls apart? You are left wondering in a daze how to pick up the pieces. This is one of those stories.

My husband, Robert, had finished a grueling work schedule of seven weeks of 7-days per week. He was physically and mentally exhausted. His usual smile and happy disposition had faded and was replaced with a pale face and dark circles under his eyes. I knew he needed rest. I suggested we rent a B&B at our favorite vacation spot, Fredericksburg, Texas. We fell in love with the quaint town, shops, wine country, and scenic roads on a previous visit. A smile returned to his face as we voraciously threw ourselves into planning our itinerary. We agreed that I would drive our SUV with our luggage, ice cooler, and snacks. Robert and his brother, Richard, would ride their motorcycles.

A beautiful sunny blue sky greeted us Friday morning when our caravan headed out on our five-hour journey to Fredericksburg. Robert told us we needed to cross the DFW metroplex highways to get out of the city before heading south towards Fredericksburg. He planned to take us on his short-cut route, which he expected would have less traffic and shorten our drive time.

Unfortunately, it had been four years since Robert last traveled his short-cut. Rapid business and residential development had multiplied the traffic and interfered with our goal to travel in tandem. It wasn't long before a series of stoplights separated Robert on his motorcycle from Richard and me. Robert pulled into a shopping center and waited for us. It was soon the least of our worries as the road turned into a brutal stretch of potholes, and rows of construction barriers confronted us for as far as we could see.

The a/c was forcefully blowing cold air on my face did not alleviate the stress I felt. Beads of sweat dripped down my nose and onto my cheeks. The road narrowed significantly. There was a four-foot drop on my right-side lane, where bulldozers pushed dirt and created various shapes of cloud monsters, which blew across the road and blurred the road ahead of me. In my rear-view mirror, miles of bumper-to-bumper traffic threatened to push me even tighter into the miles of traffic stretching ahead of me. I felt my entire body tense up in response to the cortisol pumping through my body, and my heart raced. Our options to take a different route at this point looked bleak. I groaned as it was apparent that the construction and traffic had us boxed in with no way out.

Richard and I became separated in the thick construction dust while Robert faded over the hill ahead of us. We were barely an hour from home, and I felt exasperated and exhausted. We had several more hours before we would arrive in Fredericksburg. I pulled the SUV into a shopping center, waiting for Richard. Within about five minutes, I breathed a sigh of relief as Richard appeared. He stopped and, with a frustrating tone, queried, "What next?" I pulled out my cell phone and called Robert with an emotional plea, "Where are you?"

He chuckled slightly, trying to sound cheerful, "Where are you?"

I pleaded, "We need a plan to get us out of this traffic."

Robert agreed, and he quickly suggested how to find him, and once again, we rallied down the road.

Sadly, two more stops and arguments about Robert driving too fast, and Richard and I were going too slow. The third time we stopped at a 7-11 and agreed each of us would drive the remaining three hours at our chosen speed and meet at Hondo's Mexican restaurant in town. Regretfully, our morning joy had faded.

We were soon in Texas Hill country, with beautiful rolling hills, limestone bluffs, pink granite boulders, scrub oak, and prickly pear as we approached a favorite tourist stop, Enchanted Rock. This landmark was a good sign, as I knew we were about 20 minutes from Fredericksburg.

When we arrived at Hondo's, we headed to the outdoor patio in anticipation of live entertainment. I had fingers-crossed that there would be live music to cheer us up. We plunked down into metal chairs with a table set under the biggest ceiling fan. When the waitress came, I enthusiastically ordered a Mayor's margarita and beef tacos, and Robert and Richard ordered a bucket of Shiner beer and fajitas. We were all quiet. I looked at Robert's face, which was fire red from the wind and the heat. He looked sad, and my heart sank. I looked at Richard's face, dusty from the ride, and mustache turned down in a grimace. The smile on my face had also disappeared. I felt a wave of despair and disappointment. The start of our happy adventure this morning had quickly spoiled. I was tired and hot and couldn't think of anything positive to say. The heat in the air was sweltering and didn't improve our dispositions. We all agreed we wouldn't wait for live entertainment. We were anxious to get to the B&B and settled for the evening. The sourness of the day lingered between us.

My excitement grew as we drove down Main Street headed for our turn-off to or Butterfly B&B. As I pulled the SUV into the driveway and stopped, I clapped my hands with glee to see the idyllic cottage with its long-covered porch and swing seating. The house was painted white with light blue and burgundy trim, surrounded by giant oak trees with their protective canopy of shade. Robert and Richard talked excitedly about the covered driveway where they could park their motorcycles out of the sun.

The inside of the house was as charming as the outside. The long dining room table could easily seat ten people. The two bedrooms were each decorated with fancy quilts and antique furnishings. In the living room, a large fireplace beckoned with seating on the sofa and the love seat. For entertainment, there was a television and stereo system with CDs from the '50s and '60s, including the popular entertainer Dean Martin, known for his flair for Italian songs. A quaint white gazebo with a table and four chairs sat in the center of a large green lawn and well-manicured backyard. It was that night when we sat in the gazebo listening to the dizzy whirl of the ceiling fan under the ghoulish yellow light bulb that Morelli appeared.

Robert and Richard drank Shiner beers, and I sipped on a watermelon margarita. I chided Robert for having driven too fast today and not waiting for Richard and me. Robert defended himself with pleas that it was not his fault, that he was going the speed limit. Richard also grumbled that Robert drove too fast. We were all tired and grumpy. I was immersed in my thoughts when I thought I heard Robert say something about Morelli to Richard. I was quick to jump into the conversation, "Who is Morelli?" I asked with a touch of jealousy. I've never heard you talk about Morelli before. Is this a woman or a man?"

I turned to Richard and asked, "Have you ever heard of this Morelli person before?"

Richard looked a little quizzical but responded, "Well, maybe."

I pleaded again, "So Robert, tell me about Morelli."

Robert responded, "Morelli is a man. You don't have to worry about him. He's a good old Italian-American guy like Dean Martin, 'the King of Cool,' and he shows up occasionally, right Richard?"

This time Richard seemed more animated and chuckled, "Yeah, now I remember. As you said, you never know when he will show up."

I felt slightly better with Richard's confirmation that Morelli was a man. I inquired, "When can I meet this Morelli?"

Robert looked at Richard and said, "Well, if you insist on meeting him, I guess you could meet him now."

Richard laughed at Robert's outlandish response, and I knew something was not right with this conversation. "How can that be possible? How would this Morelli person even know we are here in Fredericksburg at this B&B?"

Robert replied with a grin, "Well, he's magical and shows up whenever you need a friend."

Richard laughed even harder, and I couldn't figure out what was going on. Robert comforted me, "Kim, I am sure you will agree with Richard and me when you meet Morelli that he is humorously likable."

"Okay," I said reluctantly.

Robert pulled the fourth empty chair at the table next to me and then stood up and said, "Morelli, have a seat next to Kim and enjoy the evening with us."

Now Robert and Richard were both laughing exuberantly while my mouth hung open. "Hey, what's going on?" I said in bewilderment.

Robert explained, "Kim, I think we needed a little lighter heart this evening, and I thought that the introduction of Morelli would be interesting to you. I know how much you like to meet new people and ask them lots of questions. This evening is a great time for you to meet Morelli."

Now I started to laugh, understanding that Morelli is Robert's imaginary friend. I decided to play along. "Well, delighted to meet you, Mr. Morelli." The conversations continued the rest of the evening, with all of us asking a series of unbelievable made-up questions and associated comments with Morelli sparked continuous laughter and the joy of being together.

In the morning, while sipping my coffee, I curiously asked Robert, "How did you come up with the name 'Morelli' on the spot?"

Robert laughed softly, "Kim, you have to admit, occasionally when you are distracted or lost in your thoughts, you don't always hear the full conversation resulting in something you make up known as *Kim-isms*."

"Yes, I confess what you say is true." Robert continued explaining, "Last night I was talking to Richard about wanting to do more writing, and you imagined you heard me say, Morelli. How you got to that name is still a mystery, but I suspect, since we had a few drinks, perhaps Morelli was the combination of my not speaking succinctly enough and you not paying attention. This combination resulted in you creating the name 'Morelli,' then Richard and I embellished the story."

I closed my eyes, winced, and replied, "Yes, you could be right about that." Robert burst into a roaring laugh now as I retorted, "So to be clear, you never said Morelli?"

Robert smiled again, "No, I did not create Morelli. You did."

It was true; the imaginary Morelli saved the day! The sour emotions and the frustration of the tedious drive evaporated that evening and returned us to our feelings of joy and love for each other. Morelli has continued to be a beloved friend of the family who appears in unexpected circumstances to calm rough waters.

The fabrication of Morelli reminded us that evening how we wasted precious time on the frustrations of the day.

Morelli brought us full circle with laughter, to embrace the oneness of the day and our relationship with each other, returning us to where we started that day, with feelings of joy and excitement.

We filled our remaining vacation days with kindness and with laughter. We enjoyed a scenic bus tour of local wineries, delicious breakfast at Rathskeller's, dinner at Crossroads Saloon, and heaping scoops of homemade chocolate ice cream from Clear River Ice Cream. Ironically, our Fredericksburg "Morelli" vacation is one of our most reminisced.

Morelli is a refreshing reminder that even when difficult circumstances confront us with disappointment and fatigue, the human soul can naturally seek the harmony of oneness and the lighter side of life. We need to be willing to recognize the signs and be ready to embrace them.

Bio

Kim Pence grew up in rural Wisconsin, where her best friends were her Barbie doll, Philips record player, Beatles records, her mom's manual Remington typewriter, and inspirational books. After graduating from the University of Wisconsin Stevens Point, she moved to the suburbs of the big city of Chicago and started her career in corporate America. One of those jobs inspired her to trade long, cold winter weather for the warmer climate and sunshine in Richardson, Texas. She worked in the high-tech industry in roles supporting strategic and tactical learning, technical training development, organizational leadership management, cybersecurity training and certification credentials.

She managed multi-million-dollar technical training curriculum projects with eLearning, virtual and leader-led classes. As Kim enters the second half of her life, she is excited to return to two of her childhood friends, typing and the love of inspirational books. Kim's passion is continuous learning and a desire to blog, write inspirational stories, and take breathtaking photographs that resonate with the heart and focus on the healing power of gratitude, kindness, forgiveness, humility, and love. Life is not always easy, but we have the choice to turn adversity into hope and grace. Connect with Kim at
kim.pence2020@gmail.com.

Fog Rising Off Water
By Vanessa Plimley

By nature, I'm that bounce-out-of-bed, irritatingly-happy morning person. So when my husband or family see me stagger to the freezer for another icepack, puffy-eyed and hair in disarray, they know I am deep in the migraine hole. It is a hazy landscape filled with the murmur of missed audiobook chapters, toast for nausea, and long hours of zero thought, with my head in a vice.

Severe chronic migraines are the legacy of a case of the mosquito disease Zika gone awry, giving me encephalitis. Now with weather pressure changes, I am curled up in a dark room. Winters in North America are tough.

Yet, as I slowly climb out of a multi-day attack, I feel reborn to the world.

My senses return, the cobwebs in my mind slowly dissipate like fog rising off water. I blink like an owlet, gazing around in wonder, rolling wrists and ankles, each creaky joint stiff from lying in bed so long.

Seeking comfort, my hand reaches out for my dogs' rump to lay in a perfect divot on her thigh. She studies me with concerned eyes and a wagging tail. *Is it time?* She seems to ask with hope brimming in her gaze.

"Yes, my pup, it's time."

Tea first, then walk and sniff the wind, listen to music and feel the sun on our faces.

She can sense my energy. A burble, rising like a geyser, the need to burst out into the world after days entangled in a cotton sheet cocoon.

Her full name is Coquita Muneca Flores Mendes (Coco for short.) Our Nicaraguan beach mutt, born under a satellite dish, at a surf spot. She was a gift from the caretaker and perhaps one of the most important gifts I have ever received. I dreamt her to me at the perfect time in my life.

She was two when I fell sick and incredibly smart. After working with a service dog trainer to teach her to alert me when a migraine is pending, she has become my constant companion, my extra limb.

Coco is forever nosing me to put down the phone, close the computer and be present in the moment. She is my reminder to get outside and play, to savor moments, and go look at the world with curiosity.

Grinning at me with her tongue lolling, we leave the house, walking across our yard to the shorn cornfields, winter smells upon the wind.

We follow a farmer's dirt track and wind our way up a rolling hill. Poking our noses in large burrows of unseen forest creatures, their homes built in tree and rock islands floating in a sea of grass.

With the sun upon my face and arms wide with palms to the sky, I take in the light and clean, crisp air, open space to unfurl my heart and mind.

I close my eyes as one of my favorite songs begins to play in my earbuds. I feel blessed to have the ability to travel in my mind through music, especially when challenged by current health circumstances, a pandemic, and an unknown future.

The song is one I listen to almost every day in our heart home of Nicaragua, the chosen country we spend our time in, between work contracts. While my body stands in a field in central Pennsylvania, my mind is instantly standing on our beach.

My heart wrenches, but a wide smile spreads across my face. I imagine my feet in the cool morning sand, the warm tide washing up around my ankles, as my feet sink deeper.

I taste the salt on my tongue, the salt and pepper smells of the tropics fill the humid air, a hint of flowers mixed with the smoke of burning cane fields.

I do a slow twirl, and I can see the glassy molten colors of dawn on the sea. A flock of pelicans skim in flight only a meter above the waves, wingtips almost graze the water as they glide so silently, searching for breakfast just below the surface.

I look down once more at the beautiful ripples in the sand at low tide, colorful ribbons of light and shadow. Hidden sand dollars bubble from just beneath, sunken just out of sight from hunting egrets and sandpipers. Artistic patterns cover the beach as the small crabs have excavated balls of sand from their holes, pushed out in spreading swirls to create endless unique designs.

Coco runs gleefully, chasing the small fish stuck in the tide pools, her tail whipping back and forth, triangle ears so erect, her concentration focused. Her dog pack of friends rush down the beach to gather her for a chase of the horses feeding in the neighbors' field. They run and leap, rolling and tussling as they chase each other back through the shoreline.

A perfect symphony of colors and sounds wrap me in the beginning of a new day. Tears run down my cheeks as my soul longs desperately for the sea.

I open my eyes, somewhat shocked to know we are back standing in the field, winter chill caressing my face.

With a deep breath and slow sigh, I acknowledge the heaviness and grief for the fight I will be up against this winter, never knowing when multiple days will be lost in a week. My body feels rather haggard and beat up as the migraine hangover still clings. Gone are the pain-free summer days filled with exploding energy and a clear mind.

Once a year, I allow myself a good ugly cry and cling to Coco. This year it was sobbing in a parking lot and then over dinner where my incredible and steadfast husband held my hands, love brimming in his eyes, while he gave me a good old pep talk.

A new day dawned. I pulled up my big girl pants and very quickly counted all the blessings in my life, with the new motto of two words. *Just try.*

With that thought, we continue our walk as a red-tailed hawk leaps silently from a branch above. We study her flight path as she glides out to circle over the field. I wonder what she sees with her sharp, luminous eyes, what she hears creeping in the grass below?

Coco snuffles in holes and tears by me at top speed, with a stick she throws excitedly in the air. She wears her bright orange vest, as deer hunting rifle season is in full swing. It matches the orange wool hat of mine, to make sure we are seen from hidden tree stands in the bordering woods.

As we return home, I play catch up on life. Laundry and house cleaning, working on a writing project, and the steps to return to online coaching work. I realize creativity and patience will be needed to somehow execute these with the challenges of this current reality.

I have begun a practice of "fluid discipline." A list of things to get done in a day, week, or month, sits on my table to peck away at when possible.

Today, however, there is a deep need within me to play hooky from it all and go fly fishing.

With gear quickly thrown in the truck, Coco assumes her co-pilot position in the front seat. As thoughts roll by with the passing landscape, I reflect on how much our current life is a vast change from our ice and rock climbing days of living in the Canadian Rockies. After beating up my body in both work and play, I sought new ways to get outside, with fewer injuries.

Our first year in Pennsylvania, Coco and I were exploring a hiking trail near a beautiful stream. Two gentlemen sat behind their vehicles in the parking lot, chatting in camp chairs while sipping a morning coffee. After assembling their fly fishing gear, they split up to their own secret pools on the water. When we returned to my truck a few hours later, they were back in their chairs sporting wide grins and a beer in hand.

I thought to myself, *when I retire, this will be my sport.* Very quickly, that changed to, *why wait?* My body pleaded for a new activity that would lead me into the outdoors, to explore new terrain and water, without the expense of hurting my body.

Pulling up the truck to my first choice of river access, we find the parking lot empty. Giving Coco a scratch and the stay command, she curls up in a sunbeam on the front seat, as she casts me a rather unimpressed look. Fishing is her favorite sport, but at this particular spot, she will scare the fish away with her energetic minnow hunting on the edge of the stream.

Setting up my gear is intentionally slow as I smirk to myself, chanting my fishing mantra. *Take your time, tie good knots, crimp your hooks, breathe.*

An impish grin spreads across my face as I pull on waders and boots, what I call my fun pants, as they remind me of being a kid, pulling on a snowsuit to roll around in a fresh snowfall.

Wading into the stream brings equally calm and anticipation. A landscape shimmers with possibility and the gifts of nature. A doe stares from between the trees on the far shore, flicking her tail, before silently vanishing into the woods. An eagle circles high above in the searing blue sky as tiny midges flit in sunbeams, a hint of how I may entice the sleek, shadowy creatures below. I sing to the fish, send prayers down the river to my friends across the sea; it is river meditation at its finest.

Yet as any angler knows, the zen moments on a river are finite. It is a roller coaster of emotions mixed with the exasperation of tangled lines, of sneaky trees that snag line and fly, and the utter frustration of seeing fish appear just below the surface and the lack of the correct fly or knowledge to land it.

All my vexation is worth it in the glorious moment; it all comes together. To set the hook, let it play, and bring it close enough to scoop the most beautiful fish in the world into my net.

With wet hands, I quickly take out the hook to admire its stunning colors. Each fish so incredibly unique in color and pattern. From sunset-colored streaked sides to leopard spots or skin swathed in orange and green. What a gift to watch it powerfully swim back into the shadows, immediately hidden by its perfectly shaded body.

Anyone within hearing distance will know when I have landed a fish, my loud hooting and happy dance on the river is inevitable.

Content with a day outside, Coco and I make our way home smelling of the wild and water.

I ponder the gifts that an illness or injury can bring. The inevitable life balance of light and dark, of struggle and peace.

For this effervescent woman, I am forced to rest my body. To make the absolute most of my days when not in bed. To have deep empathy for others dealing with their own struggle and feeling so blessed with a warm house, bed, supportive husband, and furry companion. Such deep gratitude fills my heart for the love of friends and family.

We arrive home for a quiet dinner with my husband and some cards.

This simple day leaves me content, full of prayers for clear skies, and with patience and diligence, we will find a cure sometime in the future.

For now, I can dream of beautiful trout, the sun on the water, the quiet forest, and birds soaring above in a wide and open sky.

Bio

A friend once wrote, "Vanessa has the mind of an explorer and the soul of a poet." She has a deep passion for life and the desire to help others create and live one full of meaning. When not in migraine land, Vanessa is a surfer, angler, and happy soul on holiday. When able, she is an enthusiastic life coach, author, and virtual personal trainer. She splits her time between North America and Nicaragua.

To read more of her adventures, check out:
stokeyourfire.wordpress.com
www.stokeyourfire.com
vanessaplimley@gmail.com

Everyday Rituals and Connectedness
By April Porter

A question that I have pondered throughout my limited time on this planet is the question of connectedness. How does one find their place in this world without a sense of connectedness? And to elaborate, how do we gain connectedness with others and the world that we live in? I cannot presume to know the answer to this question, but I do know that it is worth the wondering and is the most important question related to my evolution.

According to the Oxford dictionary, connectedness refers to the state of being joined or linked, and according to contemporary philosophies, this sometimes-overused term can refer to a state of being or as part of self-actualization and the meaning of life.

For me, connectedness is about being in the present moment, intertwined with those I love, those I work with, those I learn from and the beautiful world that we live in. If my heart is open, I know whether I am experiencing connection or not. When I am connected, I am engaged and fully in the moment. I can sense the sights, smells and sounds around me with an awareness that opens my soul to the here and now. Connectedness means I feel bonded to the moment but unattached to the outcome, and it is in this space, whether I am looking towards the blue sky or into my child's eyes, that I feel most alive.

My perception of connectedness may not be what you know to be true, but rather a rumination of my thoughts and experiences that have taken me on a journey to understand how everyday actions move me towards peace. My learning cannot be described within a linear or circular context, but more like a doodle drawing left incomplete that lives in my book of poetic memories. The doodle drawing starts on one path and ends up on the other side of the page with an unrecognizable impression used as a bookmark in my story.

Starting from here, with awareness, what I do know to be true is that every day that I am fortunate to awake, I implement seemingly simple practices or rituals that, over time, lead to what I can only describe as magical experiences. Magical in the sense that what I know deep in my heart and soul is attuned with my day to day life. Magical in a way that creates a deep knowing of who I am and my relationship with others. Magical in a way that brings forth a sense of peace for what was, what is and what will be.

Of course, this story must begin somewhere, and for me, the fragmented memories that fill my head can only visit the past in the way that one can flip through a favorite, well-loved book. Dog ears hold some of the pages in my memory, and perhaps a favorite postcard or grocery list holds others so that I can reflect upon where I have traveled from. Once I open a page, there may be a highlighted passage or underlined sentence, and these are the moments that stay with me the most. If I go as far back as I honestly can in my book of memories, there is a note on the side of the twentieth page in cursive that says, "Start here, this is who you are, this is who you must remember to be."

This note has a kindergarten report card attached to it, and the old-school report says, "April is very social and sometimes has a hard time listening to instructions. She is constantly reminded to pay attention, sit beside students that will not influence her and to listen more and talk less." I was four years old, and I loved to be around my peers. I wonder how this teacher could have helped me develop my longing for connection rather than view it as an inconvenience. I do not remember when I stopped talking, but I believe it may be shortly after the twentieth page. Other memories have dog earmarks that look tattered and soiled with tears, and although school was not the safe place to be me, my home was as uncertain as any. Doors slammed, objects thrown, and uncontrollable anger take up many of my book's beginnings. My home life was made-up of anger and indifference, and I felt a sense of childhood shame and responsibility for it all.

Other chapters have positive pages attached to them filled with bike rides, family gatherings and hugs. Some of the pages are filled with love, the love of my mother, and her mother and so on. It is not lost on me that in this book, my book of poetic memories, I am truly blessed with a story that continues. I am also very aware that negative experiences are natural to hold onto, and they maintain their spot with the unattractive dog earmarks that makes some people cringe and ask, "Why, oh why would you do that?"

When I was in my twenties, I watched a man named Gary Zukav on the Oprah Winfrey television show. I was going through a difficult time and felt a sense of deep despair and disconnection from the world. Like many young people, I felt no sense of purpose and had a lot of anxiety about the environment and human beings in general. After that show, I immediately bought Dr. Zukav's book, Seat of the Soul and read it a few times over. At this time, I could not fully grasp all of the stories he was telling, but something propelled me to keep reading. I knew in my heart that something in this book was bound to change the way I lived and perhaps replace some of the dog earmarks with some pretty and inviting page holders. They say that lessons come to you when you are ready for them, and I know that I was not entirely willing to let go. However, the seeds of hope were in the ground, and the perennials of gratitude would soon begin to flourish.

Thinking back to these memories, I would not say that growing up was always a dark and unloved path, but it was an unguided and sometimes dimly lit one. I was a latchkey teenager of the 90s with angst that could topple almost any Martha Stewart creation. I grew up with grunge music, modest plaid attire, apathetic love stories with awesome soundtracks and a strong sense of abandonment. I wrote to Marineland and canvassed for Greenpeace at a young age, but I never truly felt like I belonged. I always longed for the perfect story.

As my book went on without the heroes or triumphs that filled my head and heart, I purposefully did things every day. I began to have visions of what a genuine and joyful life meant and how letting go of anger could open the space for something else. Most mornings, I would say thank you before my feet hit my bedroom floor, and I started to recognize that I had some choice in how I felt as I woke up. I began to walk every day, and soon, I began to notice the little things around me, like the dew on the dandelions and the sound of birds singing. I slowly began to move my body and recognize my mind's connection to it, and this allowed me to remember who I was when I was four. Of course, I would be consistent with these practices and then not, overlooking the rituals that I had started. Each day went by, days turned into years, and without warning, I was thirty-five years old, almost mid-way through my story. I had earned a university degree, owned a home and was blessed with family and friends. I continued to build a life that I felt wholeheartedly connected to and a part of. Now, I realize that this does not equate to enlightenment, and I am not trying to say that my growth is the epitome of a successful life. I am merely communicating my experience with everyday rituals and that no matter what comes next, no matter how the chapters of my story play out, I am open.

As I unlearn and learn, I continue a meditation and yoga practice that may be a struggle but never a regret once I am on my mat or sitting in a comfortable seated position. I feel the poetry and the closeness of life when I am on my mat. These moments remind me of the word thank you and help me look toward my heart center for answers. It is important to note that I am not the fluffy kind of social activist, and I do not subscribe to rainbows and unicorns in my approach to a just world. I am a critical thinker and a pessimist to the core when arguing about social justice. However, I do look at life with a required optimism and know that the only way to find joy is on purpose, and the only way to find connectedness is through awareness.

As I begin to write the last part of my story, I continue to find ways to embrace peace through my daily rituals. I meditate most mornings; I continue the same morning routine every day and move through brushing my teeth with the same mindfulness as sipping a chai latte with a friend. I move my body every day through running and yoga, and I observe the good around me. I notice things to be thankful for and give them the attention that they so lovingly deserve. I let worry have just a little bit of my time before it settles in to the mud. I breathe into my emotions, no matter what I am feeling and acknowledge their right to be there. I give myself the time and space to process information, and I challenge myself to see all sides of a situation. Although there are times when I am hurt, and there are times that I hurt others, and there are moments of binge-watching a favorite show instead of tending to the task at hand, I know that my story is still a fiercely brave one that has so much left to tell.

Over time, these everyday rituals, these behaviors that are practiced repeatedly with attention, have taught me how to gain a sense of connectedness and how to remain true to who I am. These practices remind me that within the pages of my book, I can have a hand at writing and how I engage with the world is up to me. As previously stated, I do not presume to know the meaning of life or how connectedness works for everyone, but I do know that being present in any given situation has something to do with it. For me, rituals help to stay grounded and open, so I can experience connectedness with those around me and with this beautiful world that sustains us all.

Bio

April Porter is the manager of the Nipissing EarlyON, Child and Family Centre through Community Living North Bay. She has worked in the social services and education fields for over eighteen years. She leads a team of educators and is constantly learning from her team and the families that she walks with. April is a yoga and meditation practitioner, a teacher and a student, a writer and a reader. She earned her bachelor of psychology degree and her bachelor of education degree and looks forward to completing her master's degree in psychology before her fiftieth birthday. She works and lives in North Bay, Ontario, with her three children and husband, Kevin. You can email April at
ka_porter@hotmail.com.

A Box Of Chocolates
By Felicia Shaviri

"**M**y mama always said life is like a box of chocolates. You never know what you're gonna get." ~ Forrest Gump.

The first time I heard this quote while watching the film, it was as if time stood still, and I felt a ripple of goosebumps throughout my body all at once. My mind began to reflect on some of my past experiences and their outcomes, many of which I would not have predicted in my wildest dreams to turn out the way they did.

One of the most impacting periods in my life was when I was in kindergarten. We would have story-time circles where a police officer would read to the students as we gathered to form a circle on the floor of our class. During this era, we referred to police officers as "Officer Friendly." I can remember thinking how brave, strong and courageous he must be to help people who might be in trouble that he didn't even know. It meant that he cared about people, and he was willing to protect them, and that was important to me. Story-time circle with Officer Friendly was not only the best part of my day, but it was the best part of my week. I thought to myself one day, I, too, would help people like Officer Friendly have a significant effect on me. I internally made the decision that I, too, would be a police officer one day.

I would change schools three times before completing my primary education. My mother encouraged me to attend a

Catholic high school, but I knew our family was struggling financially, and I was not about to burden her with another bill. I was adamant about not going and shared with her my choice of public high schools. My mother looked into my eyes with love as she fought back the tears and said, "Okay, Lish, okay." I gave her a hug and said, "I love you, Momma, and it's going to be alright.

I did okay in school, graduated and headed to college, where I studied communication journalism with a minor in theatre. After college, I returned to Chicago, where I found myself working in a neighborhood liquor store for several months. One of the regulars came into the store and ordered a half-gallon of Grape Concord Wine. He then said, "You have a beautiful smile," and he asked me what I was doing working in a place like the liquor store. There was something about what he said that stayed with me. As I walked into our home, I stopped and glanced at the map on the wall and thought about the question the customer had asked me earlier. I then whispered to myself a promise of going to Seattle, where I would stay for a minimum of at least six months.

Living in Washington State definitely took some getting used to, especially because there is more rain than sunshine throughout the year. It is an incredibly beautiful state full of breathtaking evergreens, hiking, mountains, and the Pacific Ocean is right outside your door. I eventually landed a career with the sheriff's department, where I worked as a Corrections Deputy for more than two decades before deciding one day at the end of my shift that I would not be returning.

I had begun to have a series of what most people may refer to as a "coincidence," but that couldn't have been further from the truth for me. I decided to follow the trail with the thought of only then would I know where it would lead. Something within me had begun to change pretty rapidly; it was as if the more I allowed myself to be open to whatever would unfold during my waking hours, and there were almost always multiple gifts throughout the day.

I found myself wanting to talk to people more and found myself fascinated by both their stories and experiences. It was as if what was happening to me was happening to so many others. I allowed myself to be open to whatever would unfold during my waking hours, and there were almost always multiple gifts throughout the day.

There was so much that I was learning about myself, everyone and everything all around me. I would speak to someone at the dog park, grocery store, or just walking down the street, and we could talk for an hour. The more that I tuned into what was happening with myself, the more I could understand another. Being aware of how I show up in the world and my connection to the other is absolutely magical.

Today I am a coach in life, fitness and wellness, as well as diversity, equity and inclusion, and I absolutely love what I do! One of the first questions I often ask of anyone is, "What did you want to be when you grew up?" Some immediately respond by sharing they are doing what they set out to do and love it. Others are stumped as they try to remember and will say, "That's a good question, I'm going to have to think about that." Then, there are those who remember and I can immediately see and feel their pain of a dream deferred or completely squashed for various reasons.

I ask this question because, for most of us, we lose sight of the importance of our imagination and the boundless creativity that comes from it. One thing that I know for sure is the importance of not having any regrets and remembering that as long as you are here, you still have time.

Yes, life changes, and we make decisions that may not have been best for us in the moment. We are all essentially a box of chocolates, and we come with different textures, shades, fillings and such that carry a variety of experiences and perspectives. Let us embrace the other as they are in their uniqueness, all the while understanding that we are one.

Bio

Felicia Shaviri is on a mission to tell everyone within earshot or afar of the importance they play in the world. A former Correctional Deputy turned Best Selling Author and Transformational Coach, Felicia Believes every person can turn their life around regardless of the circumstances. "I stand fast with an unbending belief that there is always an opportunity to learn and grow with every experience. Each experience offers us endless possibilities to live the life we desire."

A native of Chicago's South Side, Felicia lives in between Seattle, WA, and Henderson, NV, with her husband and three children. Felicia is a Professional Fitness/Wellness Coach, Certified Life Coach, Voice -Over Talent, Podcast

Host, Research Assistant at DePaul University's Department of Innovation and Founder of SheRox Fitness and Wellness based out of Henderson, NV.

Things I Want to Tell You
By Lisa Sterne

T he first time I noticed it was on my fifth birthday. I had just started kindergarten, and it was almost Halloween. I sat down on the carpet for morning circle, and my teacher approached me with a crown made from construction paper. Adorned with my name and exclamation points, I was proclaimed the classroom Birthday Girl.

This was terrific. My little heart was set aflutter. As she led the morning circle, I sat up with a certain fresh 5-year-old pride, hands folded in my lap, shoes snuggly buckled against my sweater tights. It was then that I noticed it—The Glow. The Glow was that feeling of specialness, rising up over the horizon of the '80s. The Glow surrounded you when you were told that you were the "only you" there was or had ever been. This was special. You were special. This October day was made for you, and there would be cake, song, and presents at day's end.

I didn't think much of The Glow after that day. I noticed it, for sure, but I attributed it to the wonderfulness of one's birthday. The next time I noticed it, I was nine years old, and it came in a much different form. Rushing to the girls' bathroom during class was my escape from upsetting social situations I could not yet put words to. There I would stand, with the mid-morning sun streaming in through the high window, deciding whether or not to let out the tears. Inevitably, once the stillness in the room lasted long enough and offered the promise of a few more moments of sweet solitude, I would lean against the wall inside the bathroom stall and cry. I had to be quiet otherwise they would laugh again. No one could hear me.

But that was just it—all I wanted was for someone to hear me. That's when The Glow would happen again. This time, it was quiet. It didn't boast or pump its chest the way it did on my birthdays. Instead, it stayed with me, stood beside me, and listened to the words between my tears. "No. One. Likes. Me." I would heave in silence. "They think I'm weird. They hate me. I want to go home." The Glow surrounded me and warmed up my little arms. "No one understands. They say I'm just too sensitive. I need to have a thick skin. What does that even mean?"

Soon after, I would feel the familiar relief that comes after the good cry, and I'd roll off some toilet paper and wipe my eyes. My breathing would return to normal. The redness of my cheeks would disappear. I would muster up some more courage and head down the hallway back to class.

The Glow stood beside me in the girls' bathroom for years, through the ups and downs, the math homework, the science tests, the teasing, and the pulling myself deeply inward to stay small. The Glow was my support. It was my travel companion. It always understood, without a doubt, exactly what I was going through and why it hurt. It never judged. It never asked anything of me except to speak my truth in the bathroom.

Then that thing happened that happens when we grow up— we lose touch. We lose touch with those magical-feeling experiences and even forget about them. And, in my case, I absolutely sent The Glow packing once I realized I was softer than the rest of the world, easier to damage, harder to fight. Adulthood was logical. There was no time for this. Make plans, write notes, organize lists; be linear.

So, I stepped on The Glow. I stepped on it, kept my foot on it, and made myself as small as I possibly could. The world had no patience for my big emotions. They represented immaturity. It had no interest in the fact that I was an introvert; that was something I needed to get over, recover from, be finished with.

I stayed small for a good while, a few decades even. I walked the line. I finished every class, every assignment, and every degree. I was overloaded and overstimulated, but I paid it no mind; those were weaknesses to be corrected with a New Year's resolution.

In 2019, The Glow returned. Looking through my grandmother and her friends' old photo album, I came across a black and white picture of them standing in front of a building. The columns on the side of the building slowed my page-turning down, and I stared at them for a while. "Where is this? Why does this picture remind me so much of…?" and that's when I remembered. I tore open my album from my recent trip to Washington, D.C. and combed through the photos. There it was—the picture I had taken, three months prior, of the same exact side of the Lincoln Memorial that my grandmother and her friends had stood in front of.

I inspected the detail on the columns. I counted the curves in the architecture. Then I noticed the trees. "This is it!" I shouted. "I took a picture of the Lincoln Memorial from the exact angle my grandma stood for this photo with her friends. Look. There are three bushes behind them, along the side of the building. This one's tall and skinny here, and tall and skinny there! And this one was fat and wider then, and it is still fatter and wider than the other!"

The Glow was back. I was soaring. I was inspired, energetic, and filled with light. The Glow was my guide. God, my beloved grandma, my spirit guides, whatever one best identifies with. The Glow had returned to get my attention once again. And this time, it had a lot of things to tell me. First up? No more believing in nothing.

Bio

Lisa Sterne is a social justice activist and author. She has a Master's in Counseling and worked as a child therapist for 16 years. She is married, has one daughter and three cats.

The Small Things Are Everything
By Katie Tryba

Bright light pierces through the blind.
Soaking in the warm sunshine.

Breathing out a lazy yawn.
Grateful for another dawn.

Sneaking past a sleeping pup.
Drinking hot coffee in a cozy cup.

Cushy grass between my toes.
Standing barefoot with the watering hose.

Watching the beautiful flowers in bloom.
Will surely chase away anyone's gloom.

Hot days trying to stay cool.
Dripping wet from a dip in the pool.

The smell of a lingering roast.

Ordinary Oneness

Celebrating the feast with a toast.

Night creeps in while slipping into sweatpants.

Playing games at the table without any setbacks.

Laughter fills the room.

Chatting with friends on Zoom.

Falling asleep on the backrest.

Time for bed without protest.

Filled with love.

Giving thanks to up above.

To my loved ones I cling.

The small things are everything.

I loved listening to my grandpa's stories since I was a child! He was the best storyteller I knew. Grandpa had funny, sad, and tough stories. They made me laugh and cry. I tried to imagine living his life, and this made me grateful for all that I have, which inspired me to write this poem. During the 2020 pandemic, his stories gave me comfort, knowing that this is not the first time people have had to quarantine due to illness. It made me realize we will get through this just like he did. In true grandpa fashion, I will do my best to share a few of his stories to give you hope, gratitude, or maybe just a laugh.

In Wisconsin, the year 1935 was my grandpa's first year of school. Two of the neighbor girls came over to play with him and his sister. They carried a basket of wood chips to start a fire in the stove with and placed the basket behind the stove. The neighbor girls went home, and soon the house was on fire. His mom sent him to get the neighbor girls to get their mom to come help. Grandpa ran half a mile, and they all ran back with him to help. His mom was pushing dressers out the windows, but when the fire got too bad, she had to leave it. She could not find his sister and the two neighbor girls. She was so scared they got caught in the fire, but after searching found them hiding in the corner of the barn. His dad was up in the woods, and the neighbor went to get him. They all slept at the neighbor's house that night. It was the first time my grandpa had seen a toilet in the house and was afraid to use it and get it dirty. The next day they moved into a ten-by-ten-foot shack with tar paper that had not been used in years. After chasing the wood-chucks out, they spent the winter in it. They had no money, so Grandpa was so happy when he got a two-inch car for Christmas. That winter in the shack, Grandpa came down with scarlet fever and chickenpox, which they had to be quarantined for. He missed most of the first grade. Card-board signs were nailed to the shack that read, "No one goes in, and no one goes out." If they did, they had to quarantine for six weeks at a time. His dad slept in the barn all the time so they could sell their milk.

His mom had several serious operations when he was young. His dad and mom had said their goodbyes many times as she was not expected to come out of the operations, but God always brought her home again. They had no insurance, but they scrimped and saved to pay all her hospital bills without welfare.

They stayed at their grandma's when Mom was in the hospital. They separated their milk with a hand turner, which cream ran out the spout, and the skim ran out the other. They fed the skim milk to the pigs. As he got older, he thought it was funny people bought skim to drink. One time he asked Grandma what their cow's names were. She put her hands on his shoulder and said, "Buddy boy, when Grandma goes out with the boys to do chores, all the cows have a name. There is Rosy, Polly, etc. Now the boys go out in the barn alone, and all the cows have one name, sons of bitches." And this Grandma would not say "shit" even if she had a mouth full.

They built their house in 1940 and got electricity in 1943. My grandpa's mom never had an inside toilet, running water, phone, or tv before she died in 1945. His mom kissed him goodbye in the dining room before she left for the last time. They were standing by the woodstove, and he hated to see it go when his dad replaced it with a new oil heater after his mom was gone. Grandpa just turned 16 that September, and his mom made his annual birthday meal chicken and potato pancakes. It was October when she went to the hospital to remove a tumor that was not supposed to be serious, so she wanted it removed to heal before Christmas. Great-grandpa drove to the store to call my great-grandma at the hospital the night before the operation, asking if he should come down like he normally did. She said, "No, stay home with the kids so he can do chores and not miss work at the mill and that she would be alright." Well, she never came out of recovery and died at age 42. His dad always blamed himself for not being there, and this took many years off his life. It was the biggest funeral the small town had hosted yet for the young mom. Every room in the funeral home was filled with flowers, even the hardened pastor shed tears during her sermon.

Grandpa met Grandma at a dance hall and loved her the first time he saw her. She was a skinny little thing with big brown eyes. After they got married, he always teased he had to shake the blankets to find her. They got married on his boot leave from the Marines. He flew home, got married, and drove back to California with another couple all in ten days. They lived in San Diego, Capistrano, and Laguna Beach, all off base, until Grandpa got sent overseas. Then he drove Grandma home seven months pregnant and flew back. He did not get to see his first son until he was nine months old. Grandma wrote to him every day and sent a lot of pictures. When he got home, they went for a ride, and their baby howled so much he stopped at a drug store and bought his first present, a pacifier.

Grandpa's dad stayed with them on the farm in his own trailer hooked up to the milk house for electricity. He came in the house for the bathroom and supper with them every day. Grandma did his washing, and they got along wonderfully. Grandpa and his dad argued a lot since he bought the farm and wanted to do some things differently. He would go to him and say, "Dad, I want your advice, not saying I will use it," then they would both laugh. On a cold

Sunday morning in January, his dad had a heart attack at the age of 63 and dropped dead in the barn. When grandpa found him, he tried to breathe life back into his mouth, but he knew he was already dead, and he asked God to take him home to Mom.

Grandpa would always say, "What a great family we were, and we are." Growing up, my mom and her siblings worked the farm. For extra money, they would work together in the woods at night and on Sundays peeling popple, cutting, and carrying boughs. With that money, they bought their first color tv and all the camping gear so they could camp together as a family. Lots of years in their ten-by-ten-foot tent filled with sleeping bags wall to wall with their four children. This tradition continued even as I grew up. Going camping with Grandma and Grandpa was the best. My mom and I made Grandpa his favorite potato pancakes every birthday until he passed. Visiting them for a meal and playing Sheepshead cards all night was a favorite past time. Last Grandpa quote: "We sure were a close-knit family and still are today; that is what life is all about."

Bio

Katie Tryba is from central Wisconsin. She has her master's in clinical mental health counseling. Her background includes teaching special education, facilitating at a day treatment for children and adolescents, volunteer sexual assault advocate, and short stories author. She is passionate about helping others heal. You can reach Katie at tryba.katie+book@gmail.com

Pull over: Love Meets Oneness
By Joanie Veage

If I were to share with you an ordinary experience of opening your mind and heart to love, would you be interested? If I were to share with you how love can meet a deep and meaningful oneness to everything and everyone in the universe, would you keep reading? If I were to share with you how feeling and being in this crazy little thing called love meets oneness can lift your vibration and leave you a sense of incomparable bliss, would you pull over?

Today, I am love. Let me share with you what I first didn't know. And what I recently learned, experienced, and witnessed. I think you'll like it.

I didn't pull over for much of my life and missed almost everything along the way. I didn't recognize the simplicity of the Earth's beauty and its bounty. While signs were every-where, I just didn't see it, believe it, or feel it. I wasn't walking my unique path on this human experience they call life. I didn't feel I was making healthy conn-ections. I hadn't yet found my soul partner, tribe, and sisterhood. I was also an energy vampire, carrying a lot of pain, anger, and negativity that I didn't know how to shed. I do now!

While I felt no connection to people, had no tribe or family, I did feel connected to my life's work as a chef. I gave and received deep and meaningful love to and from my two soul dogs, North and Blue. And if you're reading this, maybe you know what I mean. And about oneness! I finally have clarity on that. It resonated with me when I started composing this story with love and support from my soul tribes and sisterhood. Thank you. I love you.

In 2016, I finally pulled over. That's when I found out that everything and everyone in the universe is connected. I later discovered spirituality and finally started walking my unique path and living my life on purpose. Followed by learning a thing or two about the universal energy field and its powerful invitation to create oneness and a life you love, anytime, anywhere. I have coupled this with how to use the function of one's mind and body to create a coherence between what you believe, how you feel, and your reality. You, too, can use that universal energy to transform your life's path, destiny, and loving connections to all. I changed my mind, and it changed my life. Sounds like an ordinary oneness to me. Here are a few pearls of wisdom from great sages of history.

Your beliefs carry more power than your reality.

What we think we become.

What you feel and think about most will be on its way.

Today, I am love. I want to share with you how I got there. It's not always easy, and it takes a lot of hard work, a healthy belief system, and a few conscious agreements with oneself to achieve success. Coupled with a daily meditation practice, core principles and values, empathy, compassion, and some passion. I am doing the work. Chopping some wood and weeding my garden. It's ever empowering, joyful, and free of limiting beliefs. I am also connected to a universal movement to build deep and meaningful relationships with other humans and animals. In a career I love, with a future full of unlimited opportunities and endless possibilities. I am evident on who I am, the difference I am making in the world, and the legacy I will leave on this Earth through love and oneness. Are you with me?

Believe in Love. Feel It. Send It Back to The Universe. Love is the highest energetic vibration and a state of mindfulness that one can feel and emanate. And it's everywhere. Love does not have to come from a partner. And It's not a secret language of the universe. It's in your heart and the air you breathe, the food that nourishes your body, mind, and spirit. Your connection, too, and relationships with people, nature, and the animals that love you. Birds. Insects. Flowers. Trees. Wind. The things you love doing. *Your memorabilia.* And a spiritual connection to the universal energy field at your disposal. One can harness and even send this energy to anyone, anything, anytime, anywhere. Yes, indeed.

I like to use a daily-guided heart chakra meditation and breath-work to do so. Filling my body, mind, and spirit with a high vibration of love and light. (Some call this a heart orgasm.) With a focus on my heart chakra, the color green and a bright white heart ray that I send to those I love and those in need of love. You can do this too. Even more astonishing, you can send unconditional love back to the universe. And to your past experiences, the present moment, and even towards future events. Do so ethically, honestly, with integrity and truth. Send yourself some unconditional love too.

It is this state of mind you can expect to embody and feel when you are in your oneness, and this crazy little thing called love, exuberant health and vitality. A feeling of heaven on Earth. An abundance of joy. Bliss. Even better, what you expect to give and receive may be joy, freedom, and clarity. A manifestation of one's greatest desires. The universe is always conspiring to love and support you. You are one with this energy. Stay connected.

Let's talk some more about emanating this energy, then sending that energy back to the universe. Through laugher, it's contagious. Dancing and singing to invoke your guardian angels and holding hands with someone you love. Kissing. Eye gazing. Putting a sassy apron on and baking some cookies. Don't just eat the cookies, though. Smell the cookies. How sweet it is.

Nature and a connection to it meet in oneness. Can you remember how it felt to experience your first splash in a pool of water? Or how awesome it is to sing in the rain? Making a snow angel. Ice skating. Wet sand beneath your toes while walking on the beach. Hiking with your soul dogs. (I think you do.) A fiery sunset. A glowing sunrise. A total eclipse and a big blue moon. An aurora borealis. Cherry blossoms in full bloom. The feeling leaves you with an oneness to the Earth's beauty and its bounty. Be empowered.

Animals and Birds meet in oneness. We are one big pack of oneness when we have an affection for and connection to many animals and some birds. Deer, topping my wildlife list. Why, you ask? Deer are said to be messengers from God's energy. I learned this in Nara, Japan, in 2016. A sacred place where thousands of deer live in parks across the city's limits. Horses are a beautiful example of connecting and oneness. They are said to be one of the most telepathic animals. They give therapeutic relief to many suffering a broken heart or healing deeply rooted wounds and fears. They communicate on such a profound and spiritual level that it's simply magnificent. I am experiencing a magnificent connection and oneness to a mini horse named Stinger. We have that same secret language I shared with my soul dogs North and Blue. I feel Stinger's energy and love. Or how a cat can lift you with a belly of laughter? What can I say here? They're a little sassy. Or a little sweet. Sometimes both. Cats can promise you constant entertainment and laughter. And if you don't have a dog, deer, horse, or cat yourself, try volunteering at a shelter as I did. The connections I made there were much of the only love and oneness I gave and received for many years. Beautiful.

I'm a birder. And it's not uncommon for me to go on a bird walk when I'm in the Southern United States. Especially South Carolina, where I have seen the most beautiful birds ever. I also know this to be true. Those birds feed souls. After you attract and start feeding them, they will remain in your space; weather permitting, migration, or otherwise moved on. They will grow to depend on your food. You can rely on them for the joy they will bring you. The birds I found to be most beautiful to watch and or listen to are cardinals, blue jays, bluebirds, blackbirds, mourning doves, hummingbirds, and songbirds. Musical.

Papyrus. The greeting card company puts a little description in each card they sell. And it goes like this. The meaning behind the hummingbird: Legends say that hummingbirds float free of time, carrying our hopes for love, joy, and celebration. The hummingbird's delicate grace reminds us that life is rich, beauty is everywhere, every personal connection has meaning, and that laughter is life's sweetest creation to oneness.

Relationships. Soul Tribes and Sisterhoods. If you have a loving partner, a tribe, a sisterhood, or a gang, you are blessed. Having these connections lifts you up and feeds your soul.

Lovable things. Usually, what we most think of as priceless treasures are coupled with memorable events and experiences. Some of these treasures have been giving love for generations. They probably fill you up inside and may even heal a broken heart. Do you still have a favorite stuffed animal or doll hidden in a box, in a closet? If you do, take it out, hold it, and feel the love. Do you still have some nostalgic pictures from your childhood doing things you loved with people you love? Are they hidden in a box, in a closet? If they are, take them out, make a table book, look at it now and then and feel the love. Maybe you have a piece of jewelry, clock, cookware, apron, or a wedding gown passed down from your mother or great grandmother. Perhaps a watch or radio from your father or grandfather. Your baby or granddaughter's first holiday ornament. A pair of running shoes that catapulted your beloved husband across the finish line of his first half marathon. Your great grandfather's purple heart. A certification for achieving your greatest personal and professional goals. And your greatest personal triumph in fulling a dream and publishing your first, best-selling cookbook. My tribe and I know what it feels like to be in the presence, hold and use some of those treasures. They may leave you with a feeling of love and oneness.

Loving Spaces and Places. Perhaps one of my favorite things to do. And thanks to my friend, Dr. Lisa Thompson, and her books, *Sacred Soul Spaces* and *Sacred Soul Love*, I learned how to create harmony in my home environment that feels like love, and I was attracting the right connections, relationships; with a profound knowing and oneness that can transform your life for the better. My focus on creating this energy is always using color therapy, plants, smells, pictures, and light. This book changed my perspective and brought me great love and joy.

It's no coincidence when you think of a beloved friend and colleague of 30 years, and her favorite song starts playing on the radio. You have an angelic experience at your darkest hour. Crave a piece of your grandmother's lemon meringue pie, and your neighbor brings you a slice. The door on your job closes, and an even better one opens up. You find your lost cat after two years. Or when a breakup is a blessing in disguise. Ex-boyfriends call you after 30 years to say they're sorry. I did you a favor. And collide with your twin flame upon opening your heart to love again.

If you're reading this book, then I bet you know that many of the events and contacts in your life are no accident. Signs are everywhere. They will love, support, guide you if you ask for them and recognize them when they show up. Maybe you're struggling to answer a situation or a life-altering decision and need a little guidance. Perhaps you miss your beloved mother more than life itself. Maybe your heart is aching as your soul dogs crossed over and are waiting so patiently for you at that rainbow bridge. Well, you are not alone. And I believe that we are all still connected through energy, love, and light. This is what you need to know.

Butterflies. Beauty is but a few of the many symbolisms and meanings of butterflies. They also represent hope, change, and transformation of a better life. They often come in synergy and are no coincidence when a spiritual rebirth is on its way. And a belief that your loved ones are nearby. Their colors represent joy and light.

Dragonflies. Also recognized on a spiritual level and seen as a sign that your loved ones or guardian angels are nearby. Also seen as very advantageous. And come at just the right time. To guide you towards a direction that serves the higher good of all. Bringing freedom, clarity, and light energy into your life. Simply ask the universe for a sign.

The universe has your back and wants for you what is only in your higher good. What you want also wants you. So, be careful what you wish for; you might just get it. Join me in using this ordinary language of the universe to connect to your higher power, love, and oneness through thought, feelings, meditation, prayer, and gratitude. Be in love with life. Be in your oneness.

Bio

I am Joanie V., a Wellness Rockstar in the kitchen. Living my life on purpose. International Best Selling Author.

Certified Institute for Integrative Nutrition Health Coach. Bachelor of Science in Holistic Nutrition to include Natural Pet Care.

Finding My Way to Living Ordinary Oneness By Dorothy Welty

G rowing up, every Sunday morning, my parents piled us into the car, and off we went to Mary Seat of Wisdom Catholic Church. In my early childhood, the mass was still being said in Latin, making the hour seem an eternity. The church was modern and stark. One of the church's only attractive features was the series of stained-glass windows along each wall. Every window had a bible verse and accompanying image. To help the time pass, I would gaze upon those windows. One window in particular always caught my attention. I don't recall the image, but I fixated on the bible verse from 1 John 4:16, "*God is love, and he* that *abides in love abides in God, and God in him.*"

My contemplation of this verse led me to believe that God was not outside of myself, but God dwelled within my loving spirit. If God was the love that resided in me, then God was the love that lived in others as well. Despite individual differences, we all were one with God through our loving spirit, and therefore, we were also one with one another. That particular stained-glass window brought me my first awareness of oneness. This sense of oneness with others and the oneness with the divine spirit within each one of us was very ordinary to me as a child. While oneness was ordinary, finding my way to living in oneness was elusive.

Both my parents were young children during the great depression and World War II. They grew up just a block apart in Park Ridge, Illinois, a lovely northwest suburb of Chicago. Their generation of young children witnessed their parents deal with bread lines and rationing. They watched many family members, neighbors, and friends lose all they had worked for as the country's resources went to supporting the war effort.

My mother grew up as an only child living among the adult experience of the great depression and World War II. She spoke of this often when I was a child, and it seemed to have made her fearful of the future. She felt my father had no business choosing to settle down in the idyllic community of Park Ridge in which he and my mother had grown up. My mother feared living in Park Ridge was beyond our means. She would perpetually emphasize that we were a paycheck away from living on the street. My mother condemned my father's decision making at every turn. I never heard my mother say "yes" to any request that involved money.

My father was the youngest of four children. My father's family was an accomplished group of individuals. My grandmother made perpetual comparisons between her children and even between her grandchildren. Even as a young child, it was evident that his family saw my father as failing to measure up to his siblings' success. Even at my father's funeral, his two living siblings referred to him as the runt of the liter. As a consequence, my father feared not being good enough, accepted, or loved. Most of all, he feared being alone.

There was constant discord between my parents during all 25 years of their marriage. My brothers, sister, and I always walked on eggshells, never knowing what, if anything at all, would trigger the next argument. With the constant arguing between my parents and the fear that permeated the household, living in ordinary oneness was not to be.

Having been conditioned throughout childhood to be fearful, I lived what I had learned. I was fearful. Overcoming the past and planning the future was more important than the present. I sought happiness rather than inner peace. I feared scarcity rather than a belief in abundance. I chose ego over vulnerability. I let my head rule my heart, using thought in an attempt to control feeling. I decided to react to life's circumstances rather than respond. Being right was more important than being. Everything I feared came to fruition, and the losses were tremendous.

The suffering I resisted persisted until I broke open. As a result, the ego fell away as vulnerability, living in the moment, inner peace, abundance, and the ability to respond emerged.

I choose love, and it has allowed me to live in oneness with others and my divine spirit.

After everything I feared became my experience, I finally surrendered to the suffering, which allowed it to pass through me. For the most part, my ego has fallen away. It is now a daily practice to live in the moment. Instead of my head ruling my heart, I employ my thoughts to serve my heart. I choose to live in love and oneness with the divine spirit that connects all living things. I relinquish a dualist view where everything is good or bad, right or wrong as dictated by thoughts in my head, in favor of embracing my heart, which is of love and being, allowing me to respond to what is.

After breaking open, I became free to create a new life seeking to live in oneness. I sought a different environment for my life to support greater harmony with my divine spirit. I searched for a new career opportunity. I remembered as a child how the mountains always drew me in. There was just something about their majesty that had me feel closer to my divine spirit, so I looked for a job in Colorado so I could be close to the mountains. I now live and work with a view of the front range.

I knew I needed to reinvent my relationship with my career. As an instructional dean, I supervise many faculty and programs at the college. To stay true to living in oneness, I seek to refrain from judgment. Instead, I strive to be a servant leader working with faculty to inspire their cooperation toward a common goal: the students' best educational interests we are all employed at the college to serve. I seek to always respond from a place of love, demonstrating respect and value for my colleagues. I look for ways to acknowledge the faculty and be responsive rather than reactive in my supervisory role.

To grow my loving spirit, I needed to return to my soul nature. For the previous 25 years, I denied my spirit while focusing on being a wife, mother, and faculty member taking care of my husband, children, and students. I had lost myself amid all the caretaking of others. As a result, I became resentful and drained. In reinventing my life, I made the nurturance of my soul a priority. Self-love fertilizes my experience of ordinary oneness. I have become one with my body through stretching, yoga, and massage. I am one with my soul through daily meditation. I am one with my creative spirit through stained-glass design, woodworking, drawing, writing, cooking, and baking. I am one with nature and the creator through walking, hiking, biking, and kayaking.

A year after moving to Colorado, my oldest son and I planned a backpacking trip to Glacier National Park in Montana. With 25-pound packs on our backs and two cans of bear spray, we hiked 40 miles up and down the mountains in five days. It was the most extraordinary sense of oneness I have ever experienced. Given I was 58 years old, a bit overweight, and not in the best shape, there was no way to embark on the adventure without remaining present in the moment with every step I took for five days. The experience was a 40-mile walking meditation being one with my breath and nature. Hiking in the mountains and living in view of the mountains fills me every day with love, grace, and hope.

Another major decision I made after moving to Colorado was to adopt my first dog from a shelter. The wonderful thing about dogs is that they live in the moment and seek to keep their owners in the moment with them. Thinking that leads to judgment is not part of a dog's repertoire. Dogs perceive and respond. My dog, Sadie, has helped provide daily practice at nonjudgment and living in the now.

This past year, the restrictions that have resulted from the Covid-19 pandemic presents everyone the opportunity to live in the simplicity of everyday love, grace, and hope.

Without the ability to go to work, plan outings, trips, and social events, the invitation is even greater to live in the present moment. It has never been easier to put the past behind, and the pandemic limits future planning.

For so many decades, I was always working to overcome the past, chasing time, and anticipating the future. I was lucky to get even six hours of sleep. It was a frantic existence, rising early to get to work, racing from work to after school activities for the children, getting home for dinner and late evening chores, and then endless grading of students' papers late at night after the children had gone to bed. There was very little stillness and savoring of the moment.

As the pandemic struck and changed everyday lives worldwide, I reflected and recognized that so much of my life had just beautifully prepared me for life under Covid-19. I had already experienced so many losses and so much suffering. Those losses and suffering broke me open to living in greater simplicity and harmony with my true self. It has not been difficult to embrace the stillness and isolation brought about by the pandemic. I have experienced many benefits. I wear less makeup, spend less time primping and wear more comfortable clothes. Working remotely allows for more flexibility in my work hours and more sleep. Homecooked meals and family dinners have returned as a focal point of the day. Long walks with my dog have become not only the daily exercise but a walking meditation as well.

Eckhart Tolle says, "Life will give you whatever experience is the most helpful for the evolution of your consciousness." In many ways, the pandemic has been helpful to the evolution of my consciousness. I believe it can be beneficial to mass consciousness as well. Despite our differences, we are one in our vulnerability to the pandemic. Even strangers have come together in a loving and compassionate response to the suffering. Humankind will be forever changed.

I will be forever changed. I continue to simplify my life. I take less for granted, and my experience of gratitude for all the abundance in my life makes every day full of ordinary oneness from which so much love, grace, and hope flow.

Bio

Dorothy Welty is a community college administrator and teacher. She holds an MS in psychology from Illinois State University. She is passionate about the power of education to change individual lives and the world in which we live. In her free time, Dorothy enjoys meditation, hiking, kayaking, writing, baking, and a variety of other creative pursuits. You can reach Dorothy at dwelty50@gmail.com.

The Practice of Collective Desire
By Thomas Workman

I t started with the Great Drought of 2020.

That's a little overdramatic. But the truth is, 2020 was a year with very little rain in the Phoenix, Arizona area that I call home. Barely a drop fell during the winter months, which are usually good for a few showers, and the summer monsoon season came and went without a single storm landing anywhere near our property. Other than one or two short passer-by dribblers, our one-acre homestead, filled with desert plants and wildlife, was left bone dry. To add to the misery, 2020 brought one of the hottest summers on record, with over 114 days of temperatures over 100 degrees and many of those days reaching 110 or higher.

Even our hardiest desert plants, known for their tolerance to the desert climate, were looking ragged. Many of our saguaro cactus were drooping, bowing their towering heads in defeat to the sun, heat, and dust.

Honestly, my first impulse was to panic, believing that my newly purchased desert garden was going to dry up and blow away. I focused on the five or six trees, succulents, and cactus that were dying in front of me and how my watering efforts had failed to save them. Feeling my failure, I began apologizing to the garden.

And that's when I heard their thoughts on the matter.

I didn't hear words or sentences. Words weren't needed. Instead, I suddenly understood a different perspective—a set of thoughts that were markedly different from my own. While I was thinking that a disaster was occurring, the plants and the entire land saw the larger cycle of life. They recognized the dry season as part of the more extensive process where death produces new life and where the collective was stronger from the contrast. There was a collective trust from the garden, along with the animals, insects, and stones, that wellness was always assured, even when the current circumstances appear to the contrary. While several plants were dying, others were thriving, having long ago accepted their choice to exist in an arid region and reveling in their hardiness to endure the drought.

My attention suddenly shifted to the many flowers that continued to bloom next to a succulent that had fallen and decayed. I felt the relationship between the dead succulent, which supplied its nutrients through the earth to the flowering bush. I sensed the active conversation deep underground as roots shared the small traces of water with other roots for the good of the whole. I even had an image of javelina, which lived in several squadrons all around us, doing his part by peeing near a flowering bush I wasn't able to water. And more than once, I felt the spirit of the indigenous peoples who called my land home many years before me, who knew of the cooperation of the collective.

We did have a shared intention for rain, and I set that intention consciously with the land. And, of course, it did eventually rain again, a good soaker several months too late for some of the plants, but deeply appreciated and celebrated by the rest. But the experience of feeling the garden's perspective made the somewhat theoretical concept of a universal consciousness much more practical and real for me.

There is no question that the current energies surrounding planet Earth at this time are ushering in a new era. Some call it the Age of Aquarius to note Jupiter and Saturn's profound alignment in Aquarius, an alignment that happens only once every 800 years. Others focus on the evolution of the human species, which is moving from third to fifth dimension consciousness.

While all these are true, for me, the greatest lesson from 2020's drought and all of the catastrophes experienced across the globe is the gift we receive when we tune into the universal mind.

Oneness is synonymous with unity, an understanding that we are all the same and want the same things, and so we should focus on our similarities rather than our differences. Oneness becomes about our cooperation rather than our division. While this is true, it misses the much more critical point about oneness: we share one universal mind, and from that one mind, we can understand a rich, multifaceted perspective about life in our universe.

We often see our thoughts as private and separate from the thoughts of others. As such, we create our own thoughts and, indeed, reality as if we were an island unto ourselves. But nothing in all the universe is disconnected from the whole. Scientists have long understood that vibrational frequencies affect one another. As vibrational beings, human vibrational frequency—generated by thought— is no different. This is why you start feeling depressed when you spend some time with other depressed people and feel energized when you are around positive, happy people.

However, our collective effect on one another's vibration is much more than affecting one another's emotions. Scientists Hunt and Schooler suggest in their *resonance theory of consciousness* that others' consciousness enhances our consciousness.[1] In other words, our thoughts resonate with the thoughts of other humans (or any form of life that generates vibration), bringing us both to greater awareness and perspective.

Together, all life forms produce a mighty river of consciousness, a universal intelligence that influences and is influenced by us. Our thoughts do not begin and end with us. They join with the thoughts and emotions of all others. We are indeed one mind, ever-expanding with the contributions of our individual and collective experiences.

As I learned from my garden, the universal mind is composed of so much more than our thoughts across the planet. All life forms from all of our collective history have added to the universal consciousness and continue to do so. Every discovery and realization since the creation of life swirls next to your conclusions about every possible topic. And in the swirling, new perspectives are born that advance and expand all life, benefitting the entire collective. Throughout human history, we've seen how the collective awareness of

---

[1] For those who share my interest in science, you can find Hunt and Schooler's article on the resonance theory of consciousness at https://www.frontiersin.org/articles/10.3389/fnhum.2019.00378/full

a need or problem leads to the discovery of a solution or improvement. And the collective awareness of several social, medical, and economic challenges experienced worldwide has already begun generating new perspectives, solutions, and improvements that will advance humanity further. I call the phenomenon "collective desire," an understanding of any circumstance from the collective whole.

History has shown us that we generate tremendous power when we set an intention as a collective. Our collective desire is far more potent than our ingenuity, determination, talent or abilities. Our thoughts become things, and we have the ability through our intention to turn universal energy into form and matter or transform any circumstance. We call this manifestation. Our collective intention is indeed powerful; it has no match and knows no bounds.

But first, we need to become tuned to universal conscious-ness. With the door now wide open for us to choose to experience fifth dimension consciousness, we have access to the universal mind more than ever. The fifth dimension promises our increased ability to sense beyond ourselves and to feel beyond our thoughts. That unique human trait, empathy, which can overwhelm the third-dimensional consciousness, becomes a shared and commonplace exper-ience in fifth-dimensional awareness.

The question is, what is the purpose of empathy? Why would our evolution include increased sensitivity to the thoughts and vibrations of others? The answer is not to make you feel as miserable as the person next to you. The answer is to gain a broader perspective and set an intention resonant with the collective. Empathy for other living forms is only a means to a much larger end. I learned this lesson from my garden this past summer. The empathy I experienced for my drought-stricken plants opened me to a larger perspective the land had as a collective. In other words, our ability to feel the joy or sorrow of another is a *prompt* to seek the larger perspective of universal consciousness, and together, form an intention that benefits us all.

For me, a deeper understanding of universal consciousness and collective desire has had a profound impact on my daily practices. Understanding that we are one mind has me now asking for larger perspectives when thinking about circumstance. My experience dealing with the COVID-19 pandemic, for example, transformed as I tuned into universal consciousness and saw the collective desire for assurance, improved immunity, and a new sense of community. From this, I discovered my role in setting the intention for cooperation, collaboration, and courage, realizing these aspects in my own life as well.

It's interesting that a by-product of collective desire is a deeper understanding of our actions and how they affect the whole. For us all to truly live in a state of oneness, we need to consider our individual choices and how they are influenced by the rich perspective of the collective whole, as discovered only through our connection to universal consciousness itself. When we understand that connection, we create the better world we all want.

Bio

Thomas Workman, Ph.D., is an intuitive channel, certified angel card reader, and crystal energy healer. He is the co-founder of Camp Joy Ranch (www.campjoyranch.com) with his husband AJ, where they channel a collective of beings they call The Guides. Tom and AJ offer workshops and programs to enhance joy in body, mind, and spirit. When not channeling, Tom works for a non-profit social science research organization in the area of health policy. He is the author of numerous academic articles and book chapters, and he is delighted to now focus his writing on his spiritual work.

I Believe You
By Martha Yancey

The weary, unwilling travelers who are my clients have forged my journey. Our paths linked; Their journey is incomplete without mine and mine, incomplete without theirs.

An applicant sets out on the Social Security Disability train after applying for benefits. The government has promised these benefits if you are diagnosed with something and can't work anymore. Board the train. Your ticket is your application. *It seems simple enough.*

The train winds and curves at high speeds. There are medical records requests, appointments to attend, forms to complete within 10 days and then silence. The train slows, nearly stopping until it speeds up again to a sudden halt, giving the applicant whiplash when they read the letter. "You are not disabled." *Not. Disabled. There must be some mistake. Did they get my medical records? Did they read them?*

Most are denied. An applicant boards the next train by filling out the appeal paperwork. The train lurches forward. Perhaps there is an engine problem, or perhaps the engineer is drunk. *This is no way to drive a train.* The train speeds forward and screeches to a halt. "You are not disabled." *Did I get on the wrong train?*

The applicant boards another train, requesting a hearing before a Social Security judge. This train is a longer ride and is promised to be a smooth ride until the end. Years after agreeing to board the initial train, finally, there will be a human to speak with. To plead with. *Surely, the judge will see my suffering. Will see that I want to work but cannot. Surely.*

Under oath and penalty of perjury, the applicant speaks into the microphone, laying bare the most personal of information. There's a box of tissues on the table for a reason. Another person, on the phone, listens in like a voyeur and then speaks. Speaks about jobs they think the applicant can do. *Surely they must have drifted off to sleep while I was speaking? I can't do any job. What are they talking about? Are they talking about me? Surely the judge will believe me.*

Then, like a ball of grandma's yarn, words are twisted and manipulated into the final product: the unfavorable decision. The train ride is over. Your ticket has expired. The words "not disabled" are soldiers in black and white who usher the applicants into a dark tunnel and onto a moving sidewalk; light can't penetrate this tunnel.

As they look back onto what was, some cry out, grieving a life lost. They are unwilling travelers on this journey. There are no guidebooks that recommend this trip. No Yelp reviews to recommend tips. Rick Steves does not do tours here.

"The claimant was not under a disability, as defined in the Social Security Act." Gaslighted. *Your version of reality is not reality.* The judge did not believe their suffering or the daily pain and struggle that was offered under oath and penalty of perjury.

The moving sidewalk through the dark tunnel has sped up; the destination: the Forgotten Valley. The judge signed the final rejection with the sentence to be served in the Forgotten Valley. Another judge has declined to review the case saying that "substantial evidence" supports the first judge's decision. *How?* It is a single direction sidewalk, and a chance to get off has passed.

Still grieving for the hope that would not be, for the chance to get off of the sidewalk, the lawyer who escorted them onto the train and through the cruel system of denials delivers a final blow: they will not be taking the case any further. *You have sixty days to appeal, and here are some names of some lawyers who might be able to take your case. If all else fails, here is a 1-800 number to a national organization that may be able to provide a referral. Best of luck to you.* Some luck would be nice.

The second chance to get off the sidewalk was not there.

Was the judge right? Am I not struggling? Am I not worthy of benefits? Do I have to be dead to qualify? The sidewalk speeds up and then stops suddenly.

The sidewalk has reached its final destination, deep into the Forgotten Valley. The soil in the Valley is fertile for poverty, depression, anxiety, physical impairments. Chronic illnesses thrive and grow in the Forgotten Valley. The fruits in the Valley are self-loathing, insecurity, insomnia, despair, doubt, distrust, and fatigue. No one chooses to be here. There's no help in the Valley.

Somehow, from the depths of the Valley, they find me. I am one of the few lawyers who take cases at this stage. There are only 60 days to file an appeal in Federal District

Court. Most lawyers who take disability cases don't handle cases at this stage, after so many denials.

Many callers are reasonably timid; other callers reveal outrage that masks uncertainty. They've been rejected four or more times. Told they aren't disabled, that their case isn't worthy, that they aren't enough. They tell me the same story. They've been diagnosed with something that interferes with their lives. It may cause pain. They are severely depressed. Once they had a good job – a great job, in fact. They would love to work, if only they could. The side effects of their medications make them unable to remember much. They don't like to go out in public anymore. They don't have many friends. They have given up everything. They don't understand why the judge was against them. They don't understand why the system is against them. They don't understand why the other lawyer wouldn't continue with their case, or they tell me the other lawyer was terrible.

These are the stories I hear almost every day. Sometimes, multiple times a day.

I hear the worst parts of their lives. I listen to their pain and suffering. I listen to them calling out from the Valley. The Forgotten Valley. Cast away from the world. Problems easier to deal with if forgotten by the healthy, the lucky, and the privileged. There is no hope in the Forgotten Valley.

Sometimes, a ray of sunshine makes it into the Forgotten Valley, but it is rare. And the light is fleeting for those who spy it. The Forgotten Valley is not limited to people who have been denied disability benefits. It warmly welcomes those who find themselves down on their luck.

The massive sides of the Forgotten Valleys are lined with Teflon with its superior non-stick quality – hard to climb up and easy to slip back, even if you make it near the top. One way out of the Forgotten Valley is to grab hope and ride its coattails while it flies out of the Forgotten Valley. Another way is to touch the edge of hope ever so slightly, which makes you confident enough to attempt to climb up the Teflon sides of the Valley. Without hope, you sign the Forgotten Valley's long-term lease.

"I believe you."

That's one of the first things that I tell people who call my office. These three simple words bring the slightest sparkle of hope. That minimal glow can give the confidence to attempt to ascend the Teflon walls.

I minister to the residents of the Forgotten Valley, but I do not stay there. There is danger in spending time in the Valley. There is danger in getting comfortable in the Valley. The Valley has the power to seize hope, to take good intentions to transform them into hopelessness. I bring canteens filled with hope, and then I leave before darkness sets in. I leave before the curfew; if you linger after curfew, you will be shut in and may never make it out.

If I find myself staying too long, I remember why I am there. I remember the secret I hold close and climb the Teflon walls, sometimes after curfew.

I was a senior in college, majoring in philosophy when my mother asked me what my plan for a job was after graduation. A job? Perhaps because my program wasn't focused on vocational training, like the engineering or business programs. My mother suggested I take the LSAT, the entry test for law school admission. I signed up for the LSAT.

I had a part-time job at a kiosk selling Native American products at the local mall. A job I got solely because the owner of the kiosk approved of my "energy." I studied for the LSAT when there were no customers, which was most of my shift.

I took the LSAT in the spring and scored in the above-average range. My father took me to tour a number of different law schools – some big, some small. I applied to a handful of them and waited. The rejection letters came one after another until the final one sealed my fate. I was not admitted to a single law school. I experience a range of emotions: sadness, embarrassment, anger, hopelessness, doubt, confusion. I found myself slipping down the sides of the walls into the Forgotten Valley. I had seen people slip down into the Valley and never return.

And so, with my father's advice, I did what no rational human would do: I picked the law school I really wanted to go to, and I called to identify the deficiencies in my application. I planned to reapply with a stronger app-lication, but I first needed to know what to add to my application or what life experiences to manufacture. Yet, no one from the admissions office would take my call.

At first, I called weekly. Then, I called every other day. Then, I called daily. For months on end, I placed a daily call to a law school that determined I was unworthy of admission. The Valley had a grip on my foot and was attempting to pull me into its cradle.

One day, the admissions director took my call. After months of leaving voice messages, I had a real human on the other end of the telephone. I did not know what to say to a real human. I was nearly speechless. After a long pause, I told her that I wanted to know the reasons that my application had been rejected. Instead of telling me what my application lacked, she said that I had been granted a faculty interview.

A faculty interview.

The Valley loosened its grip.

I appeared for a faculty interview. It was a one-on-one interview with a professor. He asked me questions about some of the essays I'd written in college and whether I knew anyone who had been to law school. We had a pleasant conversation for about 30 minutes. He thanked me for my time and dismissed me. On the way out, the admissions director told me to expect something in the mail in about a week.

A week passed, and I received nothing in the mail. I could feel the Valley tugging at my foot. I called the law school and left a message. "I had a faculty interview about 10 days ago, and I haven't received anything in the mail."

To my surprise, I received a return phone call from the admission director. "You were very persuasive. You should get your acceptance letter in the mail any day."

Acceptance letter? I was admitted to law school. *I was admitted.* I shook off the Valley. There was no way I could slip down now – hope had revealed her full light, and I walked side by side with her to the first day of class. She was my companion through graduation.

After graduation, I passed the Georgia Bar Exam on my first try. Fifteen years later, I took the California Bar Exam, the most difficult bar exam in the nation. I passed, along with 28 percent of the applicants who took the exam.

I have kept my law school admission story secret until now. I feared it would delegitimize my career – that I would be viewed as an imposter and unworthy of my title. But I now find power in my story.

Every time I find myself lingering in the Forgotten Valley, I remember why I am there. For many of the people in the Valley, I am the only person who can give them any glimmer of hope. Every other lawyer they've consulted has said they have no case. Every other lawyer has rejected them. I am the last hope. I've seen the other side and know the path to take to get out. My clients can't see the way, but I can see the way light up, bright as day.

I am a guide out of the Valley. I'm not just an attorney. I am a counselor, a pathfinder. They keep me on my path into the Valley and remind me to leave before curfew. They are my pathfinders, and I am theirs.

Bio

Martha Yancey has been practicing law since 2003. She is based in Southern California and is the author of *The Applicant's Guide to Social Security Disability*. She has helped thousands of disabled individuals get the benefits they deserve. She can be reached at martha@yanceylawoffice.com.